The Riverside Aldine Series

The Riverside Aldine Series

MELIBŒUS-HIPPONAX

THE BIGLOW PAPERS

EDITED, WITH AN INTRODUCTION, NOTES, GLOSSARY, AND COPIOUS INDEX

BY

HOMER WILBUR, A. M.

PASTOR OF THE FIRST CHURCH IN JAALAM, AND (PROSPECTIVE)
MEMBER OF MANY LITERARY, LEARNED, AND
SCIENTIFIC SOCIETIES
(*for which see page* 13.)

The ploughman's whistle, or the trivial flute,
Finds more respect than great Apollo's lute.
Quarles's Emblems, B. II. E. 8

Margaritas, munde porcine, calcâsti: en, siliquas accipe
Jac. Car. Fil. ad Pub. Leg. § 1

BOSTON
HOUGHTON, MIFFLIN AND COMPANY
New York: 11 East Seventeenth Street
The Riverside Press, Cambridge
1885

Republished by
Scholarly Press, 22929 Industrial East, St. Clair Shores, Michigan 48080

Standard Book Number 403-00235-4

Library of Congress Catalog Card Number: 70-107179

This edition is printed on a high-quality,
acid-free paper that meets specification
requirements for fine book paper referred
to as "300-year" paper

CONTENTS.

CONTENTS.

NOTE TO TITLE–PAGE.

IT will not have escaped the attentive eye that I have, on the title-page, omitted those honorary appendages to the editorial name which not only add greatly to the value of every book, but whet and exacerbate the appetite of the reader. For not only does he surmise that an honorary membership of literary and scientific societies implies a certain amount of necessary distinction on the part of the recipient of such decorations, but he is willing to trust himself more entirely to an author who writes under the fearful responsibility of involving the reputation of such bodies as the *S. Archæol. Dahom.*, or the *Acad. Lit. et Scient. Kamtschat.* I cannot but think that the early editions of Shakspeare and Milton would have met with more rapid and general acceptance, but for the barrenness of their respective title-pages; and I believe that, even now, a publisher of the works of either of those justly distinguished men would find his account in procuring their admission to the membership of learned bodies on the Continent, — a proceeding no whit more incongruous than the reversal of the judgment against Socrates, when he was already more than twenty centuries beyond the reach of antidotes, and when his memory had acquired a deserved respectability. I conceive that it was a feeling of the importance of this precaution which induced Mr. Locke to style himself " Gent." on the title-page of his Essay, as who should say to his readers that they could receive his metaphysics on the honor of a gentleman.

Nevertheless, finding that, without descending to a smaller size of type than would have been compatible with the dignity of the several societies to be named, I could not compress my intended list within the limits of a single page, and thinking, moreover, that the act would carry with it an air of decorous modesty, I have chosen to take the reader aside, as it were, into my private closet, and there not only exhibit to him the diplomas which I already possess, but also to furnish him with a prophetic vision of those which I may, without undue presumption, hope for, as not beyond the reach of human ambition and attainment. And I am the rather induced to this from the fact that my name has been unaccountably dropped from the last triennial catalogue of our beloved *Alma Mater.* Whether this is to be attributed to the difficulty of Latinizing any of those honorary adjuncts (with a complete list of which I took care to furnish the proper persons nearly a year beforehand), or whether it had its origin in any more culpable motives, I forbear to consider in this place, the matter being in course of painful investigation. But, however this may be, I felt the omission the more keenly, as I had, in expectation of the new catalogue, enriched the library of the Jaalam Athenæum with the old one then in my possession, by which means it has come about that my children will be deprived of a never-wearying winter-evening's amusement in looking out the name of their parent in that distinguished roll. Those harmless innocents had at least committed no —— but I forbear, having intrusted my reflections and animadversions on this painful topic to the safekeeping of my private diary, intended for posthumous publication. I state this fact here, in order that certain nameless individ-

uals, who are, perhaps, overmuch congratu-
lating themselves upon my silence, may know
that a rod is in pickle which the vigorous
hand of a justly incensed posterity will ap-
ply to their memories.

The careful reader will note, that, in the
list which I have prepared, I have included
the names of several Cisatlantic societies to
which a place is not commonly assigned in
processions of this nature. I have ventured
to do this, not only to encourage native am-
bition and genius, but also because I have
never been able to perceive in what way dis-
tance (unless we suppose them at the end of
a lever) could increase the weight of learned
bodies. As far as I have been able to ex-
tend my researches among such stuffed spe-
cimens as occasionally reach America, I have
discovered no generic difference between the
antipodal *Fogrum Japonicum* and the *F.
Americanum* sufficiently common in our own
immediate neighborhood. Yet, with a be-
coming deference to the popular belief, that
distinctions of this sort are enhanced in value
by every additional mile they travel, I have
intermixed the names of some tolerably dis-
tant literary and other associations with the
rest.

I add here, also, an advertisement, which, that it may be the more readily understood by those persons especially interested therein, I have written in that curtailed and otherwise maltreated canine Latin, to the writing and reading of which they are accustomed.

OMNIB. PER TOT. ORB. TERRAR. CATALOG. ACADEM. EDD.

Minim. gent. diplom. ab inclytiss. acad. vest. orans, vir. honorand. operosiss., at sol. ut sciat. quant. glor. nom. meum (dipl. fort. concess.) catal. vest. temp. futur. affer., ill. subjec., addit. omnib. titul. honorar. qu. adh. non tant. opt. quam probab. put.

⁎ *Litt. Uncial. distinx. ut Præs. S. Hist. Nat. Jaal.*

HOMERUS WILBUR, Mr., Episc. Jaalam, S. T. D. 1850, et Yal. 1849, et Neo-Cæs. et Brun. et Gulielm. 1852, et Gul. et Mar. et Bowd. et Georgiop. et Viridimont. et Columb. Nov. Ebor. 1853, et Amherst. et Watervill. et S. Jarlath. Hib. et S. Mar. et S. Joseph. et S. And. Scot. 1854, et Nashvill. et Dart. et Dickins. et Concord. et Wash. et Columbian. et Charlest. et Jeff. et Dubl. et Oxon. et Cantab. et cæt. 1855, P. U. N. C. H. et J. U. D. Gott. et Osnab. et Heidelb. 1860, et Acad. BORE US. Berolin. Soc. et SS. RR. Lugd. Bat. et Patav. et Lond. et Edinb. et Ins. Feejee. et Null. Terr. et Pekin. Soc. Hon. et S. H. S. et S. P. A. et A. A. S. et S. Humb. Univ. et S. Omn. Rer. Quarund. q. Aliar. Promov. Passamaquod. et H. P. C. et I. O. H. et A. Δ. Φ. et Π. K. P. et Φ. B. K. et Peucin. et Erosoph. et Philadelph. et

Frat. in Unit. et Σ. T. et S. Archæolog. Athen. et
Acad. Scient. et Lit. Panorm. et SS. R. H. Matrit. et
Beeloochist. et Caffrar. et Caribb. et M. S. Reg. Paris.
et S. Am. Antiserv. Soc. Hon. et P. D. Gott. et LL. D.
1852, et D. C. L. et Mus. Doc. Oxon. 1860, et M. M.
S. S. et M. D. 1854, et Med. Fac. Univ. Harv. Soc.
et S. pro Convers. Pollywog. Soc. Hon. et Higgl.
Piggl. et LL. B. 1853, et S. pro Christianiz. Moschet.
Soc., et SS. Ante-Diluv. ubiq. Gent. Soc. Hon. et Civit.
Cleric. Jaalam. et S. pro Diffus. General. Tenebr.
Secret. Corr.

INTRODUCTION.

WHEN, more than three years ago, my talented young parishioner, Mr. Biglow, came to me and submitted to my animadversions the first of his poems which he intended to commit to the more hazardous trial of a city newspaper, it never so much as entered my imagination to conceive that his productions would ever be gathered into a fair volume, and ushered into the august presence of the reading public by myself. So little are we short-sighted mortals able to predict the event! I confess that there is to me a quite new satisfaction in being associated (though only as a sleeping partner) in a book which can stand by itself in an independent unity on the shelves of libraries. For there is always this drawback from the pleasure of printing a sermon, that, whereas the queasy stomach of this generation will not bear a discourse long enough to make a separate volume, those religious and godly-minded children (those Samuels, if I may call them so) of the brain must at first lie buried in an undistinguished heap, and then get such resurrection as is vouchsafed to them, mummy-wrapt with a score of others in a cheap binding, with no other mark of distinction than the word "*Miscellaneous*" printed upon the back. Far be it from me to claim any credit for the quite unexpected popularity which I am pleased to find these bucolic strains have attained unto. If I know myself, I am measurably free from the itch of vanity ; yet I may be allowed to say that I was not backward to recognize in them a certain wild, puckery, acidulous (sometimes even verging toward that point which, in our rustic phrase, is termed *shut-eye*) flavor, not wholly unpleasing, nor unwholesome, to palates cloyed with the sugariness of tamed and cultivated fruit. It may be, also, that some touches of my own, here and there, may have led to their wider acceptance, albeit solely from my larger experience of literature and authorship.[1]

---

[1] The reader curious in such matters may refer (if he can find them) to *A Sermon preached on the Anniversary of the Dark Day; An Artillery Election Sermon; A Discourse on the Late Eclipse; Dorcas, a Funeral Sermon on the Death of Madam Submit Tidd, Relict of the late Experience Tidd, Esq.*, etc., etc.

I was at first inclined to discourage Mr. Biglow's attempts, as knowing that the desire to poetize is one of the diseases naturally incident to adolescence, which, if the fitting remedies be not at once and with a bold hand applied, may become chronic, and render one, who might else become in due time an ornament of the social circle, a painful object even to nearest friends and relatives. But thinking, on a further experience, that there was a germ of promise in him which required only culture and the pulling up of weeds from around it, I thought it best to set before him the acknowledged examples of English compositions in verse, and leave the rest to natural emulation. With this view, I accordingly lent him some volumes of Pope and Goldsmith, to the assiduous study of which he promised to devote his evenings. Not long afterwards he brought me some verses written upon that model, a specimen of which I subjoin, having changed some phrases of less elegancy, and a few rhymes objectionable to the cultivated ear. The poem consisted of childish reminiscences, and the sketches which follow will not seem destitute of truth to those whose fortunate education began in a country village. And,

first, let us hang up his charcoal portrait of
the school-dame.

" Propt on the marsh, a dwelling now, I see
    The humble school-house of my A, B, C,
    Where well-drilled urchins, each behind his tire,
    Waited in ranks the wished command to fire,
    Then all together, when the signal came,
    Discharged their *a-b abs* against the dame,
    Who, 'mid the volleyed learning, firm and calm,
    Patted the furloughed ferule on her palm,
    And, to our wonder, could detect at once
    Who flashed the pan, and who was downright
        dunce.

  There young Devotion learned to climb with ease
    The gnarly limbs of Scripture family-trees,
    And he was most commended and admired
    Who soonest to the topmost twig perspired ;
    Each name was called as many various ways
    As pleased the reader's ear on different days,
    So that the weather, or the ferule's stings,
    Colds in the head, or fifty other things,
    Transformed the helpless Hebrew thrice a week
    To guttural Pequot or resounding Greek,
    The vibrant accent skipping here and there,
    Just as it pleased invention or despair ;
    No controversial Hebraist was the Dame ;
    With or without the points pleased her the same ;
    If any tyro found a name too tough,
    And looked at her, pride furnished skill enough ;
    She nerved her larynx for the desperate thing,
    And cleared the five-barred syllables at a spring.

" Ah, dear old times ! there once it was my hap,
    Perched on a stool, to wear the long-eared cap ;
    From books degraded, there I sat at ease,
    A drone, the envy of compulsory bees."

I add only one further extract, which will possess a melancholy interest to all such as have endeavored to glean the materials of Revolutionary history from the lips of aged persons, who took a part in the actual making of it, and, finding the manufacture profitable, continued the supply in an adequate proportion to the demand.

" Old Joe is gone, who saw hot Percy goad
    His slow artillery up the Concord road,
    A tale which grew in wonder, year by year,
    As, every time he told it, Joe drew near
    To the main fight, till, faded and grown gray,
    The original scene to bolder tints gave way ;
    Then Joe had heard the foe's scared double-quick
    Beat on stove drum with one uncaptured stick,
    And, ere death came the lengthening tale to lop,
    Himself had fired, and seen a red-coat drop ;
    Had Joe lived long enough, that scrambling fight
    Had squared more nearly to his sense of right,
    And vanquished Percy, to complete the tale,
    Had hammered stone for life in Concord jail."

I do not know that the foregoing extracts ought not to be called my own rather than Mr. Biglow's, as, indeed, he maintained

stoutly that my file had left nothing of his
in them. I should not, perhaps, have felt
entitled to take so great liberties with them,
had I not more than suspected an heredi-
tary vein of poetry in myself, a very near
ancestor having written a Latin poem in
the Harvard *Gratulatio* on the accession of
George the Third. Suffice it to say, that,
whether not satisfied with such limited ap-
probation as I could conscientiously bestow,
or from a sense of natural inaptitude, I
know not, certain it is that my young friend
could never be induced to any further essays
in this kind. He affirmed that it was to
him like writing in a foreign tongue, — that
Mr. Pope's versification was like the regular
ticking of one of Willard's clocks, in which
one could fancy, after long listening, a cer-
tain kind of rhythm or tune, but which yet
was only a poverty-stricken *tick*, *tick* after
all, — and that he had never seen a sweet-
water on a trellis growing so fairly, or in
forms so pleasing to his eye, as a fox-grape
over a scrub-oak in a swamp. He added I
know not what to the effect that the sweet-
water would only be the more disfigured by
having its leaves starched and ironed out,
and that Pegāsus (so he called him) hardly

looked right with his mane and tail in curl-
papers. These and other such opinions I
did not long strive to eradicate, attributing
them rather to a defective education and
senses untuned by too long familiarity with
purely natural objects, than to a perverted
moral sense. I was the more inclined to
this leniency since sufficient evidence was
not to seek, that his verses, as wanting as
they certainly were in classic polish and
point, had somehow taken hold of the public
ear in a surprising manner. So, only setting
him right as to the quantity of the proper
name Pegasus, I left him to follow the bent
of his natural genius.

There are two things upon which it would
seem fitting to dilate somewhat more largely
in this place, — the Yankee character and
the Yankee dialect. And, first, of the Yan-
kee character, which has wanted neither open
maligners, nor even more dangerous enemies
in the persons of those unskilful painters who
have given to it that hardness, angularity,
and want of proper perspective, which, in
truth, belonged not to their subject, but to
their own niggard and unskilful pencil.

New England was not so much the colony
of a mother country, as a Hagar driven forth

into the wilderness. The little self-exiled band which came hither in 1620 came not to seek gold, but to found a democracy. They came that they might have the privilege to work and pray, to sit upon hard benches and listen to painful preachers as long as they would, yea, even unto thirty-seventhly, if the spirit so willed it. And surely, if the Greek might boast his Thermopylæ, where three hundred men fell in resisting the Persian, we may well be proud of our Plymouth Rock, where a handful of men, women, and children not merely faced, but vanquished, winter, famine, the wilderness, and the yet more invincible *storge* that drew them back to the green island far away. These found no lotus growing upon the surly shore, the taste of which could make them forget their little native Ithaca; nor were they so wanting to themselves in faith as to burn their ship, but could see the fair west wind belly the homeward sail, and then turn unrepining to grapple with the terrible Unknown.

As Want was the prime foe these hardy exodists had to fortress themselves against, so it is little wonder if that traditional feud is long in wearing out of the stock. The

wounds of the old warfare were long a-heal-
ing, and an east wind of hard times puts a
new ache in every one of them. Thrift was
the first lesson in their horn-book, pointed out,
letter after letter, by the lean finger of the
hard schoolmaster, Necessity. Neither were
those plump, rosy-gilled Englishmen that
came hither, but a hard-faced, atrabilious,
earnest-eyed race, stiff from long wrestling
with the Lord in prayer, and who had taught
Satan to dread the new Puritan hug. Add
two hundred years' influence of soil, climate,
and exposure, with its necessary result of
idiosyncrasies, and we have the present Yan-
kee, full of expedients, half-master of all
trades, inventive in all but the beautiful, full
of shifts, not yet capable of comfort, armed
at all points against the old enemy, Hunger,
longanimous, good at patching, not so care-
ful for what is best as for what will *do*, with
a clasp to his purse and a button to his
pocket, not skilled to build against Time, as
in old countries, but against sore-pressing
Need, accustomed to move the world with no
ποῦ στῶ but his own two feet, and no lever
but his own long forecast. A strange hy-
brid, indeed, did circumstance beget, here in
the New World, upon the old Puritan stock,

and the earth never before saw such mystic
practicalism, such niggard-geniality, such
calculating-fanaticism, such cast-iron-enthusi-
asm, such unwilling-humor, such close-fisted-
generosity. This new *Græculus esuriens*
will make a living out of anything. He will
invent new trades as well as tools. His
brain is his capital, and he will get education
at all risks. Put him on Juan Fernandez,
and he would make a spelling-book first, and
a salt-pan afterward. *In cœlum, jusseris,
ibit,* — or the other way either, — it is all
one, so anything is to be got by it. Yet, af-
ter all, thin, speculative Jonathan is more
like the Englishman of two centuries ago
than John Bull himself is. He has lost
somewhat in solidity, has become fluent and
adaptable, but more of the original ground-
work of character remains. He feels more
at home with Fulke Greville, Herbert of
Cherbury, Quarles, George Herbert, and
Browne, than with his modern English cou-
sins. He is nearer than John, by at least a
hundred years, to Naseby, Marston Moor,
Worcester, and the time when, if ever, there
were true Englishmen. John Bull has suf-
fered the idea of the Invisible to be very
much fattened out of him. Jonathan is con-

scious still that he lives in the world of the Unseen as well as of the Seen. To move John, you must make your fulcrum of solid beef and pudding; an abstract idea will do for Jonathan.

⁎ TO THE INDULGENT READER.

MY friend, the Reverend Mr. Wilbur, having been seized with a dangerous fit of illness, before this Introduction had passed through the press, and being incapacitated for all literary exertion, sent to me his notes, memoranda, etc., and requested me to fashion them into some shape more fitting for the general eye. This, owing to the fragmentary and disjointed state of his manuscripts, I have felt wholly unable to do; yet, being unwilling that the reader should be deprived of such parts of his lucubrations as seemed more finished, and not well discerning how to segregate these from the rest, I have concluded to send them all to the press precisely as they are.

CoLUMBUS NYE,
Pastor of a Church in Bungtown Corner.

IT remains to speak of the Yankee dialect.
And first, it may be premised, in a general
way, that any one much read in the writ-
ings of the early colonists need not be told
that the far greater share of the words and
phrases now esteemed peculiar to New Eng-
land, and local there, were brought from the
mother country. A person familiar with the
dialect of certain portions of Massachusetts
will not fail to recognize, in ordinary dis-
course, many words now quoted in English
vocabularies as archaic, the greater part of
which were in common use about the time
of the King James translation of the Bible.
Shakspeare stands less in need of a glossary
to most New Englanders than to many a na-
tive of the Old Country. The peculiarities
of our speech, however, are rapidly wearing
out. As there is no country where reading
is so universal and newspapers are so multi-
tudinous, so no phrase remains long local,
but is transplanted in the mail-bags to every
remotest corner of the land. Consequently
our dialect approaches nearer to uniformity
than that of any other nation.

The English have complained of us for
coining new words. Many of those so stig-

matized were old ones by them forgotten,
and all make now an unquestioned part of
the currency, wherever English is spoken.
Undoubtedly, we have a right to make new
words, as they are needed by the fresh as-
pects under which life presents itself here
in the New World; and, indeed, wherever
a language is alive, it grows. It might be
questioned whether we could not establish a
stronger title to the ownership of the Eng-
lish tongue than the mother-islanders them-
selves. Here, past all question, is to be its
great home and centre. And not only is it
already spoken here by greater numbers, but
with a far higher popular average of correct-
ness, than in Britain. The great writers of
it, too, we might claim as ours, were owner-
ship to be settled by the number of readers
and lovers.

As regards the provincialisms to be met
with in this volume, I may say that the
reader will not find one which is not (as I
believe) either native or imported with the
early settlers, nor one which I have not, with
my own ears, heard in familiar use. In the
metrical portion of the book, I have endeav-
ored to adapt the spelling as nearly as pos-
sible to the ordinary mode of pronunciation.

Let the reader who deems me over particular
remember this caution of Martial : —

" Quem recitas, meus est, O Fidentine, libellus ;
Sed male cum recitas, incipit esse tuus."

A few further explanatory remarks will
not be impertinent.

I shall barely lay down a few general
rules for the reader's guidance.

1. The genuine Yankee never gives the
rough sound to the *r* when he can help it,
and often displays considerable ingenuity in
avoiding it even before a vowel.

2. He seldom sounds the final *g*, a piece
of self-denial, if we consider his partiality
for nasals.   The same of the final *d*, as *han'*
and *stan'* for *hand* and *stand*.

3. The *h* in such words as *while, when,*
where, he omits altogether.

4. In regard to *a*, he shows some inconsis-
tency, sometimes giving a close and obscure
sound, as *hev* for *have*, *hendy* for *handy*, *ez*
for *as*, *thet* for *that*, and again giving it the
broad sound it has in *father*, as *hânsome* for
handsome.

5. To the sound *ou* he prefixes an *e* (hard
to exemplify otherwise than orally).

The following passage in Shakspeare he
would recite thus : —

" Neow is the winta uv eour discontent
Med glorious summa by this sun o' Yock,
An' all the cleouds thet leowered upun eour heouse
In the deep buzzum o' the oshin buried ;
Neow air eour breows beound 'ith victorious wreaths ;
Eour breused arms hung up ·fer monimunce ;
Eour starn alarums chănged to merry meetins,
Eour dreffle marches to delightful measures.
Grim-visaged war heth smeuthed his wrinkled front,
An' neow, instid o' mountin' barebid steeds
To fright the souls o' ferfle edverseries,
He capers nimly in a lady's chămber,
To the lascivious pleasin' uv a loot."

6. *Au*, in such words as *daughter* and *slaughter* he pronounces *ah*.

7. To the dish thus seasoned add a drawl *ad libitum*.

[Mr. Wilbur's notes here become entirely fragmentary. — C. N.]

a. Unable to procure a likeness of Mr. Biglow, I thought the curious reader might be gratified with a sight of the editorial effigies. And here a choice between two was offered, — the one a profile (entirely black) cut by Doyle, the other a portrait painted by a native artist of much promise. The first of these seemed wanting in expression, and in the second a slight obliquity of the visual organs has been heightened (perhaps from an over-desire of force on the part of the artist) into too close an approach to actual *strabismus*. This slight divergence in my optical apparatus from the ordinary model — however I may have been taught to regard it in the light of a mercy rather than a cross, since it enabled me to give as much of directness and personal application to my discourses as met the wants of my congregation, without risk of offending any by being supposed to have him or her in my eye (as the saying is) — seeemed yet to Mrs. Wilbur a sufficient objection to the engraving of the aforesaid painting. We read of many who either absolutely refused to allow the copying of their features, as especially did Plotinus and Agesilaus among the ancients, not to mention the more modern instánces of Scioppius Palæottus, Pinellus, Velserus, Gataker, and others, or were indifferent thereto, as Cromwell.

β. Yet was Cæsar desirous of concealing his baldness. *Per contra*, my Lord Protector's carefulness in the matter of his wart might be cited. Men generally more desirous of being *improved* in their portraits than characters. Shall probably find very unflattered likenesses of ourselves in Recording Angel's gallery.

γ. Whether any of our national peculiarities may be traced to our use of stoves, as a certain closeness of the lips in pronunciation, and a smothered smoulderingness of disposition, seldom roused to open flame? An unrestrained intercourse with fire probably conducive to generosity and hospitality of soul. Ancient Mexicans used stoves, as the friar Augustin Ruiz reports, Hakluyt, III. 468, — but Popish priests not always reliable authority.

To-day picked my Isabella grapes. Crop injured by attacks of rose-bug in the spring. Whether Noah was justifiable in preserving this class of insects?

δ. Concerning Mr. Biglow's pedigree. Tolerably certain that there was never a poet among his ancestors. An ordination hymn attributed to a maternal uncle, but perhaps a sort of production not demanding the creative faculty.

His grandfather a painter of the grandiose or Michael Angelo school. Seldom painted objects smaller than houses or barns, and these with uncommon expression.

ε. Of the Wilburs no complete pedigree.
The crest said to be a *wild boar*, whence,
perhaps, the name. (?)   A connection with
the Earls of Wilbraham (*quasi* wild boar
ham) might be made out.   This suggestion
worth following up.   In 1677, John W. m.
Expect ————, had issue, 1. John, 2. Hag-
gai, 3. Expect, 4. Ruhamah, 5. Desire.

" Hear lyes yᵉ bodye of Mrs Expect Wilber,
   Yᵉ crewell salvages they kil'd her,
   Together wᵗʰ other Christian soles eleaven,
   October yᵉ ix daye, 1707.
   Yᵉ stream of Jordan sh' as crost ore
   And now expeacts me on yᵉ other shore :
   I live in hope her soon to join ;
   Her earthlye yeeres were forty and nine."
        From Gravestone in Pekussett, North Parish.

This is unquestionably the same John who
afterward (1711) married Tabitha Hagg or
Ragg.

But if this were the case, she seems to
have died early; for only three years after,
namely, 1714, we have evidence that he
married Winifred, daughter of Lieutenant
Tipping.

He seems to have been a man of sub-
stance, for we find him in 1696 conveying
" one undivided eightieth part of a salt-

meadow " in Yabbok, and he commanded a sloop in 1702.

Those who doubt the importance of genealogical studies *fuste potius quam argumento erudiendi.*

I trace him as far as 1723, and there lose him. In that year he was chosen selectman.

No gravestone. Perhaps overthrown when new hearse-house was built, 1802.

He was probably the son of John, who came from Bilham Comit. Salop. circa 1642.

This first John was a man of considerable importance, being twice mentioned with the honorable prefix of *Mr.* in the town records. Name spelt with two *l*-s.

" Hear lyeth ye bod [*stone unhappily broken.*]
Mr. Ihon Willber [Esq.] [*I inclose this in brack-
ets as doubtful. To me it seems clear.*]
Ob't die [*illegible; looks like xviii.*] . . . iii [*prob.*
1693.]

.   .   .   .   paynt
.   .   .   deseased seinte :
A friend and [fath]er untoe all ye opreast,
Hee gave ye wicked familists noe reast,
When Sat[an bl]ewe his Antinomian blaste,
Wee clong to [Willber as a steadf]ast maste.
[A]gaynst ye horrid Qua[kers] . . .

It is greatly to be lamented that this curious epitaph is mutilated. It is said that the sacrilegious British soldiers made a target of this stone during the war of Independence. How odious an animosity which pauses not at the grave! How brutal that which spares not the monuments of authentic history! This is not improbably from the pen of Rev. Moody Pyram, who is mentioned by Hubbard as having been noted for a silver vein of poetry. If his papers be still extant, a copy might possibly be recovered.

NOTICES OF AN INDEPENDENT PRESS.

[I HAVE observed, reader, (bene- or male-volent, as it may happen,) that it is customary to append to the second editions of books, and to the second works of authors, short sentences commendatory of the first, under the title of *Notices of the Press*. These, I have been given to understand, are procurable at certain established rates, payment being made either in money or advertising patronage by the publisher, or by an adequate outlay of servility on the part of the author. Considering these things with myself, and also that such notices are neither intended, nor generally believed, to convey any real opinions, being a purely ceremonial accompaniment of literature, and resembling certificates to the various morbiferal panaceas, I conceived that it would be not only more economical to prepare a sufficient number of such myself, but also more immediately subservient to the end in view to prefix them to this our primary edition rather than await the contingency of a second, when they would seem to be of small utility. To delay attaching the *bobs* until the second attempt at flying the kite would indicate but a slender experience in that useful art. Neither has it escaped my notice, nor failed to afford me matter of reflection, that, when a circus or a caravan is about to visit Jaalam, the initial step is to send forward large and highly

ornamented bills of performance to be hung in the
bar-room and the post-office. These having been suffi-
ciently gazed at, and beginning to lose their attrac-
tiveness except for the flies, and, truly, the boys also,
(in whom I find it impossible to repress, even during
school-hours, certain oral and telegraphic correspond-
ences concerning the expected show,) upon some fine
morning the band enters in a gayly-painted wagon,
or triumphal chariot, and with noisy advertisement,
by means of brass, wood, and sheepskin, makes the
circuit of our startled village streets.   Then, as the
exciting sounds draw nearer and nearer, do I desid-
erate those eyes of Aristarchus, " whose looks were
as a breeching to a boy."   Then do I perceive, with
vain regret of wasted opportunities, the advantage of
a pancratic or pantechnic education, since he is most
reverenced by my little subjects who can throw the
cleanest summerset or walk most securely upon the
revolving cask.   The story of the Pied Piper be-
comes for the first time credible to me, (albeit con-
firmed by the Hameliners dating their legal instru-
ments from the period of his exit,) as I behold how
those strains, without pretence of magical potency,
bewitch the pupillary legs, nor leave to the pedagogic
an entire self-control.   For these reasons, lest my
kingly prerogative should suffer diminution, I pro-
rogue my restless commons, whom I also follow into
the street, chiefly lest some mischief may chance be-
fall them.   After the manner of such a band, I send
forward the following notices of domestic manufac-
ture, to make brazen proclamation, not unconscious
of the advantage which will accrue, if our little craft
cymbula sutilis, shall seem to leave port with a clip-

ping breeze, and to carry, in nautical phrase, a bone
in her mouth. Nevertheless, I have chosen, as being
more equitable, to prepare some also sufficiently ob-
jurgatory, that readers of every taste may find a dish
to their palate. I have modelled them upon actually
existing specimens, preserved in my own cabinet of
natural curiosities. One, in particular, I had copied
with tolerable exactness from a notice of one of my
own discourses, which, from its superior tone and ap-
pearance of vast experience, I concluded to have been
written by a man at least three hundred years of
age, though I recollected no existing instance of such
antediluvian longevity. Nevertheless, I afterwards
discovered the author to be a young gentleman pre-
paring for the ministry under the direction of one of
my brethren in a neighboring town, and whom I had
once instinctively corrected in a Latin quantity. But
this I have been forced to omit, from its too great
length. — H. W.]

From the *Universal Littery Universe.*

Full of passages which rivet the attention of the reader.
. . . Under a rustic garb, sentiments are conveyed which
should be committed to the memory and engraven on the heart
of every moral and social being. . . . We consider this a
unique performance. . . . We hope to see it soon introduced
into our common schools. . . . Mr. Wilbur has performed his
duties as editor with excellent taste and judgment. . . . This
is a vein which we hope to see successfully prosecuted. . . .
We hail the appearance of this work as a long stride toward
the formation of a purely aboriginal, indigenous, native, and
American literature. We rejoice to meet with an author na-
tional enough to break away from the slavish deference, too
common among us, to English grammar and orthography.

. . . Where all is so good, we are at a loss how to make extracts. . . . On the whole, we may call it a volume which no library, pretending to entire completeness, should fail to place upon its shelves.

From the *Higginbottomopolis Snapping-Turtle.*

A collection of the merest balderdash and doggerel that it was ever our bad fortune to lay eyes on. The author is a vulgar buffoon, and the editor a talkative, tedious old fool. We use strong language, but should any of our readers peruse the book, (from which calamity Heaven preserve them!) they will find reasons for it thick as the leaves of Vallumbrozer, or, to use a still more expressive comparison, as the combined heads of author and editor. The work is wretchedly got up. . . . We should like to know how much *British gold* was pocketed by this libeller of our country and her purest patriots.

From the *Oldfogrunville Mentor.*

We have not had time to do more than glance through this handsomely printed volume, but the name of its respectable editor, the Rev. Mr. Wilbur, of Jaalam, will afford a sufficient guaranty for the worth of its contents. . . . The paper is white, the type clear, and the volume of a convenient and attractive size. . . . In reading this elegantly executed work, it has seemed to us that a passage or two might have been retrenched with advantage, and that the general style of diction was susceptible of a higher polish. . . . On the whole, we may safely leave the ungrateful task of criticism to the reader. We will barely suggest, that in volumes intended, as this is, for the illustration of a provincial dialect and turns of expression, a dash of humor or satire might be thrown in with advantage. . . . The work is admirably got up. . . . This work will form an appropriate ornament to the centre-table. It is beautifully printed, on paper of an excellent quality.

From the Dekay Bulwark.

We should be wanting in our duty as the conductor of that tremendous engine, a public press, as an American, and as a man, did we allow such an opportunity as is presented to us by "The Biglow Papers" to pass by without entering our earnest protest against such attempts (now, alas! too common) at demoralizing the public sentiment. Under a wretched mask of stupid drollery, slavery, war, the social glass, and, in short, all the valuable and time-honored institutions justly dear to our common humanity, and especially to republicans, are made the butt of coarse and senseless ribaldry by this low-minded scribbler. It is time that the respectable and religious portion of our community should be aroused to the alarming inroads of foreign Jacobinism, sansculottism, and infidelity. It is a fearful proof of the wide-spread nature of this contagion, that these secret stabs at religion and virtue are given from under the cloak (*credite, posteri!*) of a clergyman. It is a mournful spectacle indeed to the patriot and Christian to see liberality and new ideas (falsely so called, — they are as old as Eden) invading the sacred precincts of the pulpit. . . . On the whole, we consider this volume as one of the first shocking results which we predicted would spring out of the late French " Revolution " (!)

From the Bungtown Copper and Comprehensive Tocsin (a tryweakly family journal).

Altogether an admirable work. . . . Full of humor, boisterous, but delicate, — of wit withering and scorching, yet combined with a pathos cool as morning dew, — of satire ponderous as the mace of Richard, yet keen as the scymitar of Saladin. . . . A work full of "mountain-mirth," mischievous as Puck and lightsome as Ariel. . . . We know not whether to admire most the genial, fresh, and discursive concinnity of the author, or his playful fancy, weird imagination, and compass of style, at once both objective and subjective. . . . We might indulge in some criticisms, but, were the author other than he is, he would be a different being. As it is, he has a wonderful *pose*, which flits from flower to flower, and bears the reader irresistibly along on its eagle pinions (like Ganymede) to the "highest heaven of invention." . . . We love a book so purely objective. . . . Many of his pictures of natural scenery have an extraordinary subjective clearness and fidelity. . . . In fine, we consider this as one of the most extraordinary volumes of this or any age. We know of no English author who could have written it. It is a work to which the proud genius of our country, standing with one foot on the Aroostook and the other on the Rio Grande, and holding up the star-spangled banner amid the wreck of matter and the crush of worlds, may point with bewildering scorn of the punier efforts of enslaved Europe. . . . We hope soon to encounter our author among those higher walks of literature in which he is evidently capable of achieving enduring fame. Already we should be inclined to assign him a high position in the bright galaxy of our American bards.

From the Saltriver Pilot and Flag of Freedom.

A volume in bad grammar and worse taste. . . . While the pieces here collected were confined to their appropriate sphere in the corners of obscure newspapers, we considered them wholly beneath contempt, but, as the author has chosen to come forward in this public manner, he must expect the lash he so richly merits. . . . Contemptible slanders. . . . Vilest Billingsgate. . . . Has raked all the gutters of our language. . . . The most pure, upright, and consistent politicians not safe from his malignant venom. . . . General Cushing comes in for a share of his vile calumnies. . . . The *Reverend* Homer Wilbur is a disgrace to his cloth. . . .

From the World-Harmonic-Æolian-Attachment.

Speech is silver: silence is golden. No utterance more Orphic than this. While, therefore, as highest author, we reverence him whose works continue heroically unwritten, we have also our hopeful word for those who with pen (from wing of goose loud-cackling, or seraph God-commissioned) record the thing that is revealed. . . . Under mask of quaintest irony, we detect here the deep, storm-tost (nigh shipwracked) soul, thunder-scarred, semarticulate, but ever climbing hopefully toward the peaceful summits of an Infinite Sorrow. . . . Yes, thou poor, forlorn Hosea, with Hebrew fire-flaming soul in thee, for thee also this life of ours has not been without its aspects of heavenliest pity and laughingest mirth. Conceivable enough! Through coarse Thersites-cloak, we have revelation of the heart, wild-glowing, world-clasping, that is in him. Bravely he grapples with the life-problem as it presents itself to him, uncombed, shaggy, careless of the "nicer proprieties," inexpert of "elegant diction," yet with voice audible enough to whoso hath ears, up there on the gravelly side-hills, or down on the splashy, Indiarubber-like salt-marshes of native Jaalam. To this soul also the *Necessity of Creating* somewhat has unveiled its awful front. If not Œdipuses and Electras and Alcestises, then in God's name Birdofredum Sawins! These also shall get born into the world, and filch (if so need) a Zingali subsistence therein, these lank, omnivorous Yankees of his. He shall paint the Seen, since the Unseen will not sit to him. Yet in him also are Nibelungen-lays, and Iliads, and Ulysses-wanderings, and Divine Comedies, — if only once he could come at them! Therein lies much, nay all; for what truly is this which we name *All*, but that which we do *not* possess? . . . Glimpses also are given us of an old father Ezekiel, not without paternal pride, as is the wont of such. A brown, parchment-hided old man of the geoponic or bucolic species, gray-eyed, we fancy, *queued* perhaps, with much weather-cunning and plentiful September-gale memories, bidding fair in good time to become the Oldest Inhabitant. After such hasty apparition, he vanishes and is seen no more. . . . Of "Rev. Homer Wilbur, A. M., Pastor of the First Church in Jaalam," we have small care to speak here. Spare touch in him of his Melesigenes namesake, save, haply, the — blindness! A tolerably caliginose, nephelegeretous elderly gentleman, with infinite faculty of sermonizing, muscularized by long practice, and excellent digestive apparatus, and, for the rest, well-meaning enough, and with small private illuminations (somewhat tallowy, it is to be feared) of his own.

To him, there, "Pastor of the First Church in Jaalam," our Hosea presents himself as a quite inexplicable Sphinx-riddle. A rich poverty of Latin and Greek, — so far is clear enough, even to eyes peering myopic through horn-lensed editorial spectacles, — but naught farther? O purblind, well-meaning, altogether fuscous Melesigenes-Wilbur, there are things in him incommunicable by stroke of birch! Did it ever enter that old bewildered head of thine that there was the *Possibility of the Infinite* in him? To thee, quite wingless (and even featherless) biped, has not so much even as a dream of wings ever come? "Talented young parishioner"? Among the Arts whereof thou art *Magister*, does that of *seeing* happen to be one? Unhappy *Artium Magister!* Somehow a Nemean lion, fulvous, torrid-eyed, dry-nursed in broad-howling sand-wildernesses of a sufficiently rare spirit-Libya (it may be supposed) has got whelped among the sheep. Already he stands wild-glaring, with feet clutching the ground as with oak-roots, gathering for a Remus-spring over the walls of thy little fold. In Heaven's name, go not near him with that fly-bite crook of thine! In good time, thou painful preacher, thou wilt go to the appointed place of departed Artillery-Election Sermons, Right-Hands of Fellowship, and Results of Councils, gathered to thy spiritual fathers with much Latin of the Epitaphial sort; thou, too, shalt have thy reward; but on him the Eumenides have looked, not Xantippes of the pit, snake-tressed, finger-threatening, but radiantly calm as on antique gems; for him paws impatient the winged courser of the gods, champing unwelcome bit; him the starry deeps, the empyrean glooms, and far-flashing splendors await.

From the Onion Grove Phœnix.

A talented young townsman of ours, recently returned from a Continental tour, and who is already favorably known to our readers by his sprightly letters from abroad which have graced our columns, called at our office yesterday. We learn from him, that, having enjoyed the distinguished privilege, while in Germany, of an introduction to the celebrated Von Humbug, he took the opportunity to present that eminent man with a copy of the "Biglow Papers." The next morning he received the following note, which he has kindly furnished us for publication. We prefer to print *verbatim*, knowing that our readers will readily forgive the few errors into which the illustrious writer has fallen, through ignorance of our language.

"HIGH-WORTHY MISTER!

"I shall also now especially happy starve, because I have more or less a work of one those aboriginal Red Men seen in which have I so deaf an interest ever taken full-worthy on the self shelf with our Gottsched to be upset.

"Pardon my in the English-speech unpractice!

"VON HUMBUG."

He also sent with the above note a copy of his famous work on "Cosmetics," to be presented to Mr. Biglow; but this was taken from our friend by the English custom-house officers, probably through a petty national spite. No doubt, it has by this time found its way into the British Museum. We trust this outrage will be exposed in all our American papers. We shall do our best to bring it to the notice of the State Department. Our numerous readers will share in the pleasure we experience at seeing our young and vigorous national literature thus encouragingly patted on the head by this venerable and world-renowned German. We love to see these reciprocations of good-feeling between the different branches of the great Anglo-Saxon race.

[The following genuine "notice" having met my eye, I gladly insert a portion of it here, the more especially as it contains a portion of one of Mr. Biglow's poems not elsewhere printed. — H. W.]

From the Jaalam Independent Blunderbuss.

. . . But, while we lament to see our young townsman thus mingling in the heated contests of party politics, we think we detect in him the presence of talents which, if properly directed, might give an innocent pleasure to many. As a proof that he is competent to the production of other kinds of poe-

try, we copy for our readers a short fragment of a pastoral by
him, the manuscript of which was loaned us by a friend.
The title of it is " The Courtin'. "

> ZEKLE crep' up, quite unbeknown,
>   An' peeked in thru the winder,
> An' there sot Huldy all alone,
>   'ith no one nigh to hender.
>
> Agin' the chimbly crooknecks hung,
>   An' in amongst 'em rusted
> The ole queen's arm thet gran'ther Young
>   Fetched back from Concord busted.
>
> The wannut logs shot sparkles out
>   Towards the pootiest, bless her!
> An' leetle fires danced all about
>   The chiny on the dresser.
>
> The very room, coz she wuz in,
>   Looked warm from floor to ceilin',
> An' she looked full ez rosy agin
>   Ez th' apples she wuz peelin'.
>
> She heerd a foot an' knowed it, tu,
>   Araspin' on the scraper, —
> All ways to once her feelins flew
>   Like sparks in burnt-up paper.
>
> He kin' o' l'itered on the mat,
>   Some doubtfle o' the seekle;
> His heart kep' goin' pitypat,
>   But hern went pity Zekle.

.   .   .   .

Satis multis sese emptores futuros libri professis, Georgius Nichols, Cantabrigiensis, opus emittet de parte gravi sed adhuc neglecta historiæ naturalis, cum titulo sequenti, videlicet:

Conatus ad Delineationem naturalem nonnihil perfectiorem Scarabœi Bombilatoris, vulgo dicti Humbug, ab Homero Wilbur, Artium Magistro, Societatis historico-naturalis Jaalamensis Præside (Secretario, Socioque (eheu!) singulo,) multarumque aliarum Societatum eruditarum (sive ineruditarum) tam domesticarum quam transmarinarum Socio — forsitan futuro.

PROEMIUM.

Lectori Benevolo S.

Toga scholastica nondum deposita, quum systemata varia entomologica, a viris ejus scientiæ cultoribus studiosissimis summa diligentia ædificata, penitus indagâssem, non fuit quin luctuose omnibus in iis, quamvis aliter laude dignissimis, hiatum magni mo-

menti perciperem. Tunc, nescio quo motu
superiore impulsus, aut qua captus dulcedine
operis, ad eum implendum (Curtius alter)
me solemniter devovi. Nec ab isto labore,
δαιμονίως imposito, abstinui antequam tracta-
tulum sufficienter inconcinnum lingua verna-
cula perfeceram. Inde, juveniliter tume-
factus, et barathro ineptiæ τῶν βιβλιοπωλῶν
(necnon " Publici Legentis ") nusquam ex-
plorato, me composuisse quod quasi placen-
tas præfervidas (ut sic dicam) homines in-
gurgitarent credidi. Sed, quum huic et alii
bibliopolæ MSS. mea submisissem et nihil
solidius responsione valde negativa in Mu-
sæum meum retulissem, horror ingens atque
misericordia, ob crassitudinem Lambertia-
nam in cerebris homunculorum istius muneris
cœlesti quadam ira infixam, me invasere.
Extemplo mei solius impensis librum edere
decrevi, nihil omnino dubitans quin " Mun-
dus Scientificus " (ut aiunt) crumenam meam
ampliter repleret. Nullam, attamen, ex agro
illo meo parvulo segetem demessui, præter
gaudium vacuum bene de Republica merendi.
Iste panis meus pretiosus super aquas lite-
rarias fæculentas præfidenter jactus, quasi
Harpyiarum quarundam (scilicet bibliopola-
rum istorum facinorosorum supradictorum)

tactu rancidus, intra perpaucos dies mihi do-
mum rediit. Et, quum ipse tali victu ali
non tolerarem, primum in mentem venit pis-
tori (typographo nempe) nihilominus solven-
dum esse. Animum non idcirco demisi, imo
æque ac pueri naviculas suas penes se lino
retinent (eo ut e recto cursu delapsas ad
ripam retrahant), sic ego Argô meam char-
taceam fluctibus laborantem a quæsitu vel-
leris aurei, ipse potius tonsus pelleque exu-
tus, mente solida revocavi. Metaphoram ut
mutem, *boomarangam* meam a scopo aber-
rantem retraxi, dum majore vi, occasione
ministrante, adversus Fortunam intorque-
rem. Ast mihi, talia volventi, et, sicut Sa-
turnus ille παιδοβόρος, liberos intellectus mei
depascere fidenti, casus miserandus, nec an-
tea inauditus, supervenit. Nam, ut ferunt
Scythas pietatis causa et parsimoniæ, pa-
rentes suos mortuos devorâsse, sic filius hic
meus primogenitus, Scythis ipsis minus man-
suetus, patrem vivum totum et calcitrantem
exsorbere enixus est. Nec tamen hac de
causa sobolem meam esurientem exheredavi.
Sed famem istam pro valido testimonio viri-
litatis roborisque potius habui, cibumque ad
eam satiandam salva paterna mea carne,
petii. Et quia bilem illam scaturientem ad

æs etiam concoquendum idoneam esse esti-
mabam, unde æs alienum, ut minoris pretii,
haberem, circumspexi. Rebus ita se haben-
tibus, ab avunculo meo Johanne Doolittle,
Armigero, impetravi ut pecunias necessarias
suppeditaret, ne opus esset mihi universita-
tem relinquendi antequam ad gradum pri-
mum in artibus pervenissem. Tunc ego, sal-
vum facere patronum meum munificum
maxime cupiens, omnes libros primæ edi-
tionis operis mei non venditos una cum pri-
vilegio in omne ævum ejusdem imprimendi
et edendi avunculo meo dicto pigneravi. Ex
illo die, atro lapide notando, curæ vocifer-
antes familiæ singulis annis crescentis eo us-
que insultabant ut nunquam tam carum pig-
nus e vinculis istis aheneis solvere possem.

Avunculo vero nuper mortuo, quum inter
alios consanguineos testamenti ejus lectio-
nem audiendi causa advenissem, erectis auri-
bus verba talia sequentia accepi : " Quoniam
persuasum habeo meum dilectum nepotem
Homerum, longa et intima rerum angusta-
rum domi experientia, aptissimum esse qui
divitias tueatur, beneficenterque ac prudenter
iis divinis creditis utatur, — ergo, motus hisce
cogitationibus, exque amore meo in illum
magno, do, legoque nepoti caro meo supra-

nominato omnes singularesque istas posses-
siones nec ponderabiles nec computabiles
meas quæ sequuntur, scilicet : quingentos
libros quos mihi pigneravit dictus Homerus,
anno lucis 1792, cum privilegio edendi et re-
petendi opus istud ' scientificum ' (quod di-
cunt) suum, si sic elegerit.   Tamen D. O. M.
precor oculos Homeri nepotis mei ita aperiat
eumque moveat, ut libros istos in bibliotheca
unius e plurimis castellis suis Hispaniensibus
tuto abscondat."

His verbis (vix credibilibus) auditis, cor
meum in pectore exsultavit.   Deinde, quo-
niam tractatus Anglice scriptus spem auc-
toris fefellerat, quippe quum studium His-
toriæ Naturalis in Republica nostra inter
factionis strepitum languescat, Latine ver-
sum edere statui, et eo potius quia nescio
quomodo disciplina academica et duo diplo-
mata proficiant, nisi quod peritos linguarum
omnino mortuarum (et damnandarum, ut
dicebat iste πανοῦργος Gulielmus Cobbett)
nos faciant.

Et mihi adhuc superstes est tota illa editio
prima, quam quasi crepitaculum per quod
dentes caninos dentibam retineo.

OPERIS SPECIMEN.

(Ad exemplum Johannis Physiophili speciminis Mona-chologiæ.)

12. S. B. *Militaris*, WILBUR. *Carnifex*, JABLONSK.
   Profanus, DESFONT.

[Male hancce speciem *Cyclopem* Fabricius
vocat, ut qui singulo oculo ad quod sui inter-
est distinguitur. Melius vero Isaacus Outis
nullum inter S. milit. S. que Belzebul (Fa-
bric. 152) discrimen esse defendit.]

Habitat civitat. Americ. austral.

Aureis lineis splendidus; plerumque tamen
sordidus, utpote lanienas valde frequentans,
fœtore sanguinis allectus. Amat quoque in-
super septa apricari, neque inde, nisi maxima
conatione, detruditur. *Candidatus* ergo po-
pulariter vocatus. Caput cristam quasi pen-
narum ostendit. Pro cibo vaccam publicam
callide mulget; abdomen enorme; facultas
suctus haud facile estimanda. Otiosus, fatu-
us; ferox nihilominus, semperque dimicare
paratus. Tortuose repit.

Capite sæpe maxima cum cura dissecto,
ne illud rudimentum etiam cerebri commune
omnibus prope insectis detegere poteram.

Unam de hoc S. milit. rem singularem no-

tavi; nam S. Guineens. (Fabric. 143) servos
facit, et idcirco a multis summa in reveren-
tia habitus, quasi scintillas rationis pæne hu-
manæ demonstrans.

24. S. B. *Criticus,* WILBUR. *Zoilus,* FABRIC. *Pyg-
mœus,* CARLSEN.

[Stultissime Johannes Stryx cum S. punc-
tato (Fabric. 64–109) confundit. Specimina
quamplurima scrutationi microscopicæ sub-
jeci, nunquam tamen unum ulla indicia
puncti cujusvis prorsus ostendentem inveni.]

Præcipue formidolosus, insectatusque, in
proxima rima anonyma sese abscondit, *we,
we,* creberrime stridens. Ineptus, segnipes.

Habitat ubique gentium; in sicco; nidum
suum terebratione indefessa ædificans. Ci-
bus. Libros depascit; sicoss præcipue seli-
gens, et forte succidum.

THE BIGLOW PAPERS.

No. I.

A LETTER

FROM MR. EZEKIEL BIGLOW OF JAALAM TO THE HON. JOSEPH T. BUCKINGHAM, EDITOR OF THE BOSTON COURIER, INCLOSING A POEM OF HIS SON, MR. HOSEA BIGLOW.

JAYLEM, june, 1846.

MISTER EDDYTER: — Our Hosea wuz down to Boston last week, and he see a cruetin Sarjunt a struttin round as popler as a hen with 1 chicking, with 2 fellers a drummin and fifin arter him like all nater. the sarjunt he thout Hosea hed n't gut his i teeth cut cos he looked a kindo 's though he 'd jest com down, so he cal'lated to hook him in, but Hosy wood n't take none o' his sarse for all he hed much as 20 Rooster's tales stuck onto his hat and eenamost enuf brass a bobbin up and down on his shoulders and figureed onto his coat and trousis, let alone wut nater hed sot in his featers, to make a 6 pounder out on.

wal, Hosea he com home considerabal
riled, and arter I 'd gone to bed I heern Him
a thrashin round like a short-tailed Bull in
fli-time. The old Woman ses she to me ses
she, Zekle, ses she, our Hosee's gut the chol-
lery or suthin anuther ses she, don't you Bee
skeered, ses I, he 's oney amakin pottery [1]
ses i, he 's ollers on hand at that ere busynes
like Da & martin, and shure enuf, cum morn-
in, Hosy he cum down stares full chizzle, hare
on eend and cote tales flyin, and sot rite of to
go reed his varses to Parson Wilbur bein he
haint aney grate shows o' book larnin him-
self, bimeby he cum back and sed the par-
son wuz dreffle tickled with 'em as i hoop
you will Be, and said they wuz True grit.

Hosea ses taint hardly fair to call 'em hisn
now, cos the parson kind o' slicked off sum
o' the last varses, but he told Hosee he did
n't want to put his ore in to tetch to the
Rest on 'em, bein they wuz verry well As
thay wuz, and then Hosy ses he sed suthin
a nuther about Simplex Mundishes or sum
sech feller, but I guess Hosea kind o' did n't
hear him, for I never hearn o' nobody o'
that name in this villadge, and I 've lived
here man and boy 76 year cum next tater

[1] *Aut insanit, aut versos facit.* — H. W.

diggin, and thair aint no wheres a kitting spryer 'n I be.

If you print 'em I wish you 'd jest let folks know who hosy's father is, cos my ant Keziah used to say it 's nater to be curus ses she, she aint livin though and he 's a likely kind o' lad.

EZEKIEL BIGLOW.

THRASH away, you 'll *hev* to rattle
    On them kittle drums o' yourn, —
'T aint à knowin' kind o' cattle
    Thet is ketched with mouldy corn ;
Put in stiff, you fifer feller,
    Let folks see how spry you be, —
Guess you 'll toot till you are yeller
    'Fore you git ahold o' me !

Thet air flag 's a leetle rotten,
    Hope it aint your Sunday's best ; —
Fact ! it takes a sight o' cotton
    To stuff out a soger's chest :
Sence we farmers hev to pay fer 't,
    Ef you must wear humps like these,
Sposin' you should try salt hay fer 't,
    It would du ez slick ez grease.

'T would n't suit them Southun fellers,
    They 're a dreffle graspin' set,

We must ollers blow the bellers
　　Wen they want their irons het ;
May be it 's all right ez preachin',
　　But *my* narves it kind o' grates,
Wen I see the overreachin'
　　O' them nigger-drivin' States.

Them thet rule us, them slave-traders,
　　Haint they cut a thunderin' swarth,
(Helped by Yankee renegaders,)
　　Thru the vartu o' the North !
We begin to think it 's nater
　　To take sarse an' not be riled ; —
Who 'd expect to see a tater
　　All on eend at bein' biled ?

Ez fer war, I call it murder, —
　　There you hev it plain an' flat ;
I don't want to go no furder
　　Than my Testyment fer that ;
God hez sed so plump an' fairly,
　　It 's ez long ez it is broad,
An' you 've gut to git up airly
　　Ef you want to take in God.

'Taint your eppyletts an' feathers
　　Make the thing a grain more right ;
'Taint afollerin' your bell-wethers
　　Will excuse ye in His sight ;
Ef you take a sword an' dror it,
　　An' go stick a feller thru,

Guv'ment aint to answer for it,
    God 'll send the bill to you.

Wut 's the use o' meetin-goin'
    Every Sabbath, wet or dry,
Ef it 's right to go amowin'
    Feller-men like oats an' rye?
I dunno but wut it 's pooty
    Trainin' round in bobtail coats, —
But it 's curus Christian dooty
    This ere cuttin' folks's throats.

They may talk o' Freedom's airy
    Tell they 're pupple in the face, —
It 's a grand gret cemetary
    Fer the barthrights of our race;
They jest want this Californy
    So 's to lug new slave-states in
To abuse ye, an' to scorn ye,
    And to plunder ye like sin.

Aint it cute to see a Yankee
    Take sech everlastin' pains
All to git the Devil's thankee,
    Helpin' on 'em weld their chains?
Wy, it 's jest ez clear ez figgers,
    Clear ez one an' one make two,
Chaps thet make black slaves o' niggers
    Want to make wite slaves o' you.

Tell ye jest the eend I 've come to
   Arter cipherin' plaguy smart,
An' it makes a handy sum, tu,
   Any gump could larn by heart;
Laborin' man an' laborin' woman
   Hev one glory an' one shame,
Ev'y thin' thet 's done inhuman
   Injers all on 'em the same.

'Taint by turnin' out to hack folks
   You 're agoin' to git your right,
Nor by lookin' down on black folks
   Coz you 're put upon by wite ;
Slavery aint o' nary color,
   'Taint the hide thet makes it wus,
All it keers fer in a feller
   'S jest to make him fill its pus.

Want to tackle *me* in, du ye ?
   I expect you 'll hev to wait ;
Wen cold led puts daylight thru ye
   You 'll begin to kal'late ;
S'pose the crows wun't fall to pickin'
   All the carkiss from your bones,
Coz you helped to give a lickin'
   To them poor half-Spanish drones ?

Jest go home an' ask our Nancy
   Wether I 'd be sech a goose
Ez to jine ye, — guess you 'd fancy
   The etarnal bung wuz loose !

She wants me fer home consumption,
    Let alone the hay 's to mow. —
Ef you 're arter folks o' gumption,
    You 've a darned long row to hoe.

Take them editors thet 's crowin'
    Like a cockerel three months old, —
Don't ketch any on 'em goin',
    Though they *be* so blasted bold ;
Aint they a prime set o' fellers ?
    'Fore they think on 't they will sprout,
(Like a peach that' s got the yellers,)
    With the meanness bustin' out.

Wal, go 'long to help 'em stealin'
    Bigger pens to cram with slaves,
Help the men that 's ollers dealin'
    Insults on your fathers' graves ;
Help the strong to grind the feeble,
    Help the many agin the few,
Help the men thet call your people
    Witewashed slaves an' peddlin' crew !

Massachusetts, God forgive her,
    She 's akneelin' with the rest,
She, thet ough' to ha' clung fer ever
    In her grand old eagle-nest ;
She thet ough' to stand so fearless
    Wile the wracks are round her hurled,
Holdin' up a beacon peerless
    To the oppressed of all the world !

Haint they sold your colored seamen?
  Haint they made your env'ys wiz?
Wut 'll make ye act like freemen?
  Wut 'll git your dander riz?
Come, I 'll tell ye wut I 'm thinkin'
  Is our dooty in this fix,
They 'd ha' done 't ez quick ez winkin'
  In the days o' seventy-six.

Clang the bells in every steeple,
  Call all true men to disown
The tradoocers of our people,
  The enslavers o' their own;
Let our dear old Bay State proudly
  Put the trumpet to her mouth,
Let her ring this messidge loudly
  In the ears of all the South: —

" I 'll return ye good fer evil
  Much ez we frail mortils can,
But I wun't go help the Devil
  Makin' man the cus o' man;
Call me coward, call me traiter,
  Jest ez suits your mean idees, —
Here I stand a tyrant-hater,
  An' the friend o' God an' Peace! "

Ef I 'd *my* way I hed ruther
  We should go to work an' part, —
They take one way, we take t'other, —
  Guess it would n't break my heart;

THIS kind o' sogerin' aint a mite like our October trainin',

A chap could clear right out from there ef 't only looked like rainin'.

An' th' Cunnles, tu, could kiver up their shappoes with bandanners,

An' send the insines skootin' to the bar-room with their banners,

(Fear o' gittin' on 'em spotted,) an' a feller could cry quarter

Ef he fired away his ramrod arter tu much rum an' water.

Recollect wut fun we hed, you 'n I an' Ezry Hollis,

Up there to Waltham plain last fall, ahavin' the Cornwallis ? [1]

This sort o' thing aint *jest* like thet, — I wish thet I wuz furder, — [2]

Nimepunce a day fer killin' folks comes kind o' low fer murder,

(Wy I 've worked out to slarterin' some fer Deacon Cephas Billins,

An' in the hardest times there wuz I ollers tetched ten shillins,)

There 's sutthin' gits into my throat thet makes it hard to swaller,

It comes so nateral to think about a hempen collar ;

[1] i hait the Site of a feller with a muskit as I du pizn But their *is* fun to a cornwallis I aint agoin' to deny it. — H. B.

[2] he means Not quite so fur i guess. — H. B.

It 's glory, — but, in spite o' all my tryin' to git
    callous,
I feel a kind o' in a cart, aridin' to the gallus.
But wen it comes to *bein'* killed, — I tell ye I
    felt streaked
The fust time ever I found out wy baggonets wuz
    peaked ;
Here 's how it wuz : I started out to go to a fan-
    dango,
The sentinul he ups an' sez, " That 's furder 'an
    you can go."
" None o' your sarse," sez I ; sez he " Stan'
    back ! " " Aint you a buster ? "
Sez I, " I 'm up to all thet air, I guess I 've ben
    to muster ;
I know wy sentinuls air sot ; you aint agoin' to
    eat us ;
Caleb haint no monopoly to court the seenoreetas ;
My folks to hum air full ez good ez hisn be, by
    golly ! "
An' so ez I wuz goin' by, not thinkin' wut would
    folly,
The everlastin' cus he stuck his one - pronged
    pitchfork in me
An' made a hole right thru my close ez ef I wuz
    an in'my.

Wal, it beats all how big I felt hoorawin' in ole
    Funnel
Wen Mister Bolles he gin the sword to our
    Leftenant Cunnle,

Browne, desire its establishment, inasmuch as the acquirement of that sacred tongue would thereby be facilitated. I am aware that Herodotus states the conclusion of Psammeticus to have been in favor of a dialect of the Phrygian. But, beside the chance that a trial of this importance would hardly be blessed to a Pagan monarch whose only motive was curiosity, we have on the Hebrew side the comparatively recent investigation of James the Fourth of Scotland. I will add to this prefatory remark, that Mr. Sawin, though a native of Jaalam, has never been a stated attendant on the religious exercises of my congregation. I consider my humble efforts prospered in that not one of my sheep hath ever indued the wolf's clothing of war, save for the comparatively innocent diversion of a militia training. Not that my flock are backward to undergo the hardships of *defensive* warfare. They serve cheerfully in the great army which fights even unto death *pro aris et focis*, accoutred with the spade, the axe, the plane, the sledge, the spelling-book, and other such effectual weapons against want and ignorance and unthrift. I have taught them (under God) to esteem our human institutions as but tents of a night, to be stricken whenever Truth puts the bugle to her lips and sounds a march to the heights of wider-viewed intelligence and more perfect organization. — H. W.]

MISTER BUCKINUM, the follerin Billet was writ hum by a Yung feller of our town that wuz cussed fool enuff to goe atrottin inter Miss Chiff arter a Drum and fife. it

ain't Nater for a feller to let on that he 's
sick o' any bizness that He went intu off his
own free will and a Cord, but I rather cal'-
late he 's middlin tired o' voluntearin By this
Time.   I bleeve u may put dependunts on
his statemence.   For I never heered nothin
bad on him let Alone his havin what Parson
Wilbur cals a *pongshong* for cocktales, and
he ses it wuz a soshiashun of idees sot him
agoin arter the Crootin Sargient cos he wore
a cocktale onto his hat.

his Folks gin the letter to me and i shew
it to parson Wilbur and he ses it oughter
Bee printed.   send It to mister Buckinum,
ses he, i don't ollers agree with him, ses he,
but by Time,[1] ses he, I *du* like a feller that
ain't a Feared.

I have intusspussed a Few refleckshuns
hear and thair. We 're kind o' prest with
Hayin.

Ewers respecfly
HOSEA BIGLOW.

[1] In relation to this expression, I cannot but think that
Mr. Biglow has been too hasty in attributing it to me.
Though Time be a comparatively innocent personage to
swear by, and though Longinus in his discourse Περὶ Ὕψους
has commended timely oaths as not only a useful but sub-
lime figure of speech, yet I have always kept my lips free
from that abomination. *Odi profanum vulgus*, I hate your
swearing and hectoring fellows. — H. W.

Man hed ough' to put asunder
  Them thet God has noways jined,
An' I should n't gretly wonder
  Ef there 's thousands o' my mind.

[The first recruiting sergeant on record I conceive to have been that individual who is mentioned in the Book of Job as *going to and fro in the earth, and walking up and down in it.* Bishop Latimer will have him to have been a bishop, but to me that other calling would appear more congenial. The sect of Cainites is not yet extinct, who esteemed the first-born of Adam to be the most worthy, not only because of that privilege of primogeniture, but inasmuch as he was able to overcome and slay his younger brother. That was a wise saying of the famous Marquis Pescara to the Papal Legate, that *it was impossible for men to serve Mars and Christ at the same time.* Yet in time past the profession of arms was judged to be κατ' ἐξοχήν that of a gentleman, nor does this opinion want for strenuous upholders even in our day. Must we suppose, then, that the profession of Christianity was only intended for losels, or, at best, to afford an opening for plebeian ambition? Or shall we hold with that nicely metaphysical Pomeranian, Captain Vratz, who was Count Königsmark's chief instrument in the murder of Mr. Thynne, that the Scheme of Salvation has been arranged with an especial eye to the necessities of the upper classes, and that " God would consider a *gentleman* and deal with him suitably to the condition and profession he had placed him in " ? It may be said of us all, *Exemplo plus quam ratione vivimus.* — H. W.]

NO. II.

A LETTER

FROM MR. HOSEA BIGLOW TO THE HON. J. T. BUCK-
INGHAM, EDITOR OF THE BOSTON COURIER, COV-
ERING A LETTER FROM MR. B. SAWIN, PRIVATE
IN THE MASSACHUSETTS REGIMENT.

[THIS letter of Mr. Sawin's was not originally
written in verse. Mr. Biglow, thinking it peculiarly
susceptible of metrical adornment, translated it, so
to speak, into his own vernacular tongue. This is
not the time to consider the question, whether rhyme
be a mode of expression natural to the human race.
If leisure from other and more important avocations
be granted, I will handle the matter more at large
in an appendix to the present volume. In this place
I will barely remark, that I have sometimes noticed
in the unlanguaged prattlings of infants a fondness
for alliteration, assonance, and even rhyme, in which
natural predisposition we may trace the three de-
grees through which our Anglo-Saxon verse rose to
its culmination in the poetry of Pope. I would not
be understood as questioning in these remarks that
pious theory which supposes that children, if left
entirely to themselves, would naturally discourse
in Hebrew. For this the authority of one experi-
ment is claimed, and I could, with Sir Thomas

(It's Mister Secondary Bolles,[1] thet writ the
        prize peace essay ;
Thet's wy he did n't list himself along o' us, I
        dessay,)
An' Rantoul, tu, talked pooty loud, but don't
        put *his* foot in it,
Coz human life's so sacred thet he's principled
        agin' it, —
Though I myself can't rightly see it's any wus
        achokin' on 'em
Than puttin' bullets thru their lights, or with a
        bagnet pokin' on 'em ;
How dreffle slick he reeled it off, (like Blitz at
        our lyceum
Ahaulin' ribbins from his chops so quick you
        skeercely see 'em,)
About the Anglo-Saxon race (an' saxons would
        be handy
To du the buryin' down here upon the Rio
        Grandy),
About our patriotic pas an' our star-spangled
        banner,
Our country's bird alookin' on an' singin' out ho-
        sanner,
An' how he (Mister B. himself) wuz happy fer
        Ameriky, —
I felt, ez sister Patience sez, a leetle mite hister-
        icky.

---

1 the ignerant creeter means Sekketary; but he ollers stuck
to his books like cobbler's wax to an ile-stone. — H. B.

I felt, I swon, ez though it wuz a dreffle kind o'
    privilege
Atrampin' round thru Boston streets among the
    gutter's drivelage ;
I act'lly thought it wuz a treat to hear a little
    drummin',
An' it did bonyfidy seem millanyum wuz acomin'
Wen all on us got suits (darned like them wore
    in the state prison)
An' every feller felt ez though all Mexico wuz
    hisn.[1]

This 'ere's about the meanest place a skunk
    could wal diskiver
(Saltillo's Mexican, I b'lieve, fer wut we call
    Saltriver).
The sort o' trash a feller gits to eat does beat all
    nater,
I 'd give a year's pay fer a smell o' one good
    bluenose tater ;
The country here thet Mister Bolles declared to
    be so charmin'
Throughout is swarmin' with the most alarmin'
    kind o' varmin'.

[1] it must be aloud that thare's a streak o' nater in lovin'
sho, but it sartinly is 1 of the curusest things in nater to see
a rispecktable dri goods dealer (deekon off a chutch mayby)
a riggin' himself out in the Weigh they du and struttin'
round in the Reign aspilin' his trowsis and makin wet goods
of himself. Ef any thin's foolisher and moor dicklus than
militerry gloary it is milishy gloary. — H. B.

He talked about delishis froots, but then it wuz a
    wopper all,

The holl on't 's mud an' prickly pears, with here
    an' there a chapparal;

You see a feller peekin' out, an', fust you know,
    a lariat

Is round your throat an' you a copse, 'fore you
    can say, " Wut air ye at ? " [1]

You never see sech darned gret bugs (it may not
    be irrelevant

To say I 've seen a *scarabœus pilularius* [2] big ez
    a year old elephant,)

The rigiment come up one day in time to stop a
    red bug

From runnin' off with Cunnle Wright, — 't wuz
    jest a common *cimex lectularius.*

One night I started up on eend an' thought I wuz
    to hum agin,

I heern a horn, thinks I it 's Sol the fisherman
    hez come agin,

His bellowses is sound enough, — ez I 'm a livin'
    creeter,

I felt a thing go thru my leg, — 't wuz nothin'
    more 'n a skeeter !

[1] these fellers are verry proppilly called Rank Heroes, and
the more tha kill the ranker and more Herowick tha bekum.
— H. B.

[2] it wuz "tumblebug" as he Writ it, but the parson put
the Latten instid. i sed tother maid better meeter, but he
said tha was eddykated peepl to Boston and tha would n't
stan' it no how. idnow as tha *wood* and idnow *as* tha wood.
— H. B.

Then there 's the yaller fever, tu, they call it here
    el vomito, —
(Come, thet wun't du, you landcrab there, I tell
    ye to le' *go* my toe !
My gracious ! it 's a scorpion thet 's took a shine
    to play with 't,
I dars n't skeer the tarnal thing fer fear he 'd run
    away with 't.)
Afore I come away from hum I hed a strong per-
    suasion
Thet Mexicans wor n't human beans,[1] — an ou-
    rang outang nation,
A sort o' folks a chap could kill an' never dream
    on 't arter,
No more 'n a feller 'd dream o' pigs thet he hed
    hed to slarter ;
I 'd an idee thet they were built arter the darkie
    fashion all,
An' kickin' colored folks about, you know, 's a
    kind o' national ;
But wen I jined I wor n 't so wise ez thet air
    queen o' Sheby,
Fer, come to look at 'em, they aint much diff'rent
    from wut we be,
An' here we air ascrougin' 'em out o' thir own
    dominions,
Ashelterin' 'em, ez Caleb sez, under our eagle's
    pinions,

---

1 he means human beins, that 's wut he means. i spose he
kinder thought tha wuz human beans ware the Xisle Poles
comes from. — H. B.

Wich means to take a feller up jest by the slack
 o' 's trowsis
An' walk him Spanish clean right out o' all his
 homes an' houses ;
Wal, it does seem a curus way, but then hooraw
 fer Jackson !
It must be right, fer Caleb sez it 's reg'lar Anglo-
 saxon.
The Mex'cans don't fight fair, they say, they piz'n
 all the water,
An' du amazin' lots o' things, thet is n't wut they
 ough' to ;
Bein' they haint no lead, they make their bullets
 out o' copper
An' shoot the darned things at us, tu, wich Caleb
 sez aint proper ;
He sez they 'd ough' to stan' right up an' let us
 pop 'em fairly,
(Guess wen he ketches 'em at thet he 'll hev to
 git up airly,)
Thet our nation 's bigger 'n theirn an' so its
 rights air bigger,
An' thet it 's all to make 'em free thet we air
 pullin' trigger,
The Anglo Saxondom's idee 's abreakin' 'em to
 pieces,
An' thet idee 's thet every man doos jest wut he
 damn pleases ;
Ef I don't make his meanin' clear, perhaps in
 some respex I can,

I know thet "every man" don't mean a nigger
    or a Mexican;
An' there's another thing I know, an' thet is ef
    these creeturs,
Thet stick an Anglosaxon mask onto State-prison
    feeturs,
Should come to Jaalam Centre fer to argify an'
    spout on 't,
The gals 'ould count the silver spoons the minnit
    they cleared out on 't.

This goin' ware glory waits ye haint one agree-
    able feetur,
An' ef it wor n't fer wakin' snakes, I 'd home
    agin short meter ;
O, would n't I be off, quick time, ef 't wor n't
    thet I wuz sartin
They 'd let the daylight into me to pay me fer
    desartin !
I don't approve o' tellin' tales, but jest to you I
    may state
Our ossifers aint wut they wuz afore they left
    the Bay-state ;
Then it wuz "Mister Sawin, sir, you 're middlin'
    well now, be ye ?
Step up an' take a nipper, sir; I 'm dreffle glad
    to see ye ; "
But now it 's " Ware 's my eppylet? here, Sawin,
    step an' fetch it !
An' mind your eye, be thund'rin' spry, or, damn
    ye, you shall ketch it ! "

Wal, ez the Doctor sez, some pork will bile so,
        but by mighty,
Ef I hed some on 'em to hum, I 'd give 'em
        linkumvity,
I 'd play the rogue's march on their hides an'
        other music follerin' ——
But I must close my letter here, for one on 'em 's
        a hollerin'.
These Anglosaxon ossifers, — wal, taint no use
        ajawin',
I 'm safe enlisted fer the war,
                Yourn,
                    BIRDOFREDOM SAWIN.

[Those have not been wanting (as, indeed, when
hath Satan been to seek for attorneys?) who have
maintained that our late inroad upon Mexico was
undertaken, not so much for the avenging of any na-
tional quarrel, as for the spreading of free institu-
tions and of Protestantism. *Capita vix duabus An-
ticyris medenda!* Verily I admire that no pious ser-
geant among these new Crusaders beheld Martin
Luther riding at the front of the host upon a tamed
pontifical bull, as, in that former invasion of Mexico,
the zealous Diaz (spawn though he were of the
Scarlet Woman) was favored with a vision of St.
James of Compostella, skewering the infidels upon
his apostolic lance. We read, also, that Richard of
the lion heart, having gone to Palestine on a similar
errand of mercy, was divinely encouraged to cut the
throats of such Paynims as refused to swallow the

bread of life (doubtless that they might be there-
after incapacitated for swallowing the filthy gobbets
of Mahound) by angels of heaven, who cried to the
king and his knights, *Seigneurs, tuez! tuez!* provi-
dentially using the French tongue, as being the only
one understood by their auditors. This would argue
for the pantoglottism of these celestial intelligences,
while on the other hand, the Devil, *teste* Cotton Ma-
ther, is unversed in certain of the Indian dialects.
Yet must he be a semeiologist the most expert mak-
ing himself intelligible to every people and kindred
by signs ; no other discourse, indeed, being need-
ful, than such as the mackerel-fisher holds with his
finned quarry, who, if other bait be wanting, can by
a bare bit of white rag at the end of a string capti-
vate those foolish fishes. Such piscatorial oratory is
Satan cunning in. Before one he trails a hat and
feather, or a bare feather without a hat ; before an-
other, a Presidential chair, or a tidewaiter's stool, or
a pulpit in the city, no matter what. To us, dan-
gling there over our heads, they seem junkets dropped
out of the seventh heaven, sops dipped in nectar, but,
once in our mouths, they are all one, bits of fuzzy
cotton.

This, however, by the way. It is time now *revo-
care gradum.* While so many miracles of this sort,
vouched by eyewitnesses, have encouraged the arms
of Papists, not to speak of those *Dioscuri* (whom we
must conclude imps of the pit) who sundry times
captained the pagan Roman soldiery, it is strange
that our first American crusade was not in some such
wise also signalized. Yet it is said that the Lord
hath manifestly prospered our armies. This opens

the question, whether, when our hands are strengthened to make great slaughter of our enemies, it be absolutely and demonstratively certain that this might is added to us from above, or whether some Potentate from an opposite quarter may not have a finger in it, as there are few pies into which his meddling digits are not thrust. Would the Sanctifier and Setter-apart of the seventh day have assisted in a victory gained on the Sabbath, as was one in the late war? Or has that day become less an object of his especial care since the year 1697, when so manifest a providence occurred to Mr. William Trowbridge, in answer to whose prayers, when he and all on shipboard with him were starving, a dolphin was sent daily, "which was enough to serve 'em ; only on *Saturdays* they still catched a couple, and on the *Lord's Days* they could catch none at all"? Haply they might have been permitted, by way of mortification, to take some few sculpins (those banes of the salt-water angler), which unseemly fish would, moreover, have conveyed to them a symbolical reproof for their breach of the day, being known in the rude dialect of our mariners as *Cape Cod Clergymen.*

It has been a refreshment to many nice consciences to know that our Chief Magistrate would not regard with eyes of approval the (by many esteemed) sinful pastime of dancing, and I own myself to be so far of that mind, that I could not but set my face against this Mexican Polka, though danced to the Presidential piping with a Gubernatorial second. If ever the country should be seized with another such mania *de propagandâ fide,* I think it would be wise to fill our bombshells with alternate copies of the Cambridge Platform and the Thirty-nine Articles, which would produce a mixture of the highest explosive power, and to wrap every one of our cannonballs in a leaf of the New Testament, the reading of which is denied to those who sit in the darkness of Popery. Those iron evangelists would thus be able to disseminate vital religion and Gospel truth in quarters inaccessible to the ordinary missionary. I have seen lads, unimpregnate with the more sublimated punctiliousness of Walton, secure pickerel, taking their unwary *siesta* beneath the lily-pads too nigh the surface, with a gun and small shot. Why not, then, since gunpowder was unknown to the Apostles (not to enter here upon the question whether it were discovered before that period by the Chinese), suit our metaphor to the age in which we live, and say *shooters* as well as *fishers* of men?

I do much fear that we shall be seized now and then with a Protestant fervor, as long as we have neighbor Naboths whose wallowings in Papistical mire excite our horror in exact proportion to the size and desirableness of their vineyards. Yet I rejoice that some earnest Protestants have been made by this war, — I mean those who protested against it. Fewer they were than I could wish, for one might imagine America to have been colonized by a tribe of those nondescript African animals the Aye-Ayes, so difficult a word is *No* to us all. There is some malformation or defect of the vocal organs, which either prevents our uttering it at all, or gives it so thick a pronunciation as to be unintelligible. A mouth filled with the national pudding, or watering in expectation thereof, is wholly incompetent to this refractory monosyllable. An abject and herpetic Public Opinion is the Pope, the Anti-Christ, for us to protest against *e corde cordium.* And by what College of Cardinals is this our God's-vicar, our binder and looser, elected? Very like, by the sacred conclave of Tag, Rag, and Bobtail, in the gracious atmosphere of the grog-shop. Yet it is of this that we must all be puppets. This thumps the pulpit-cushion, this guides the editor's pen, this wags the senator's tongue. This decides what Scriptures are canonical, and shuffles Christ away into the Apocrypha. According to that sentence fathered upon Solon, Οὕτω δημόσιον κακὸν ἔρχεται οἴκαδ᾽ ἑκάστῳ. This unclean spirit is skilful to assume various shapes. I have known it to enter my own study and nudge my elbow of a Saturday under the semblance of a wealthy member of my congregation. It were a great blessing, if every particular of what in the sum we call popular sentiment could carry about the name of its manufacturer stamped legibly upon it. I gave a stab under the fifth rib to that pestilent fallacy, — "Our country, right or wrong," — by tracing its original to a speech of Ensign Cilley at a dinner of the Bungtown Fencibles. — H. W.]

WHAT MR. ROBINSON THINKS.

[A FEW remarks on the following verses will not be out of place. The satire in them was not meant to have any personal, but only a general, application. Of the gentleman upon whose letter they were intended as a commentary, Mr. Biglow had never heard till he saw the letter itself. The position of the satirist is oftentimes one which he would not have chosen, had the election been left to himself. In attacking bad principles, he is obliged to select some individual who has made himself their exponent, and in whom they are impersonate, to the end that what he says may not, through ambiguity, be dissipated *tenues in auras.* For what says Seneca? *Longum iter per præcepta, breve et efficace per exempla.* A bad principle is comparatively harmless while it continues to be an abstraction, nor can the general mind comprehend it fully till it is printed in that large type which all men can read at sight, namely, the life and character, the sayings and doings, of particular persons. It is one of the cunningest fetches of Satan, that he never exposes himself directly to our arrows, but, still dodging behind this neighbor or that acquaintance, compels us to wound him through them, if at all. He holds our affections as hostages, the while he patches up a truce with our conscience.

Meanwhile, let us not forget that the aim of the

true satirist is not to be severe upon persons, but only upon falsehood, and, as Truth and Falsehood start from the same point, and sometimes even go along together for a little way, his business is to follow the path of the latter after it diverges, and to show her floundering in the bog at the end of it. Truth is quite beyond the reach of satire. There is so brave a simplicity in her, that she can no more be made ridiculous than an oak or a pine. The danger of the satirist is, that continual use may deaden his sensibility to the force of language. He becomes more and more liable to strike harder than he knows or intends. He may be careful to put on his boxing-gloves, and yet forget, that, the older they grow, the more plainly may the knuckles inside be felt. Moreover, in the heat of contest, the eye is insensibly drawn to the crown of victory, whose tawdry tinsel glitters through that dust of the ring which obscures Truth's wreath of simple leaves. I have sometimes thought that my young friend, Mr. Biglow, needed a monitory hand laid on his arm, — *aliquid sufflaminandus erat.* I have never thought it good husbandry to water the tender plants of reform with *aqua fortis*, yet, where so much is to do in the beds, he were a sorry gardener who should wage a whole day's war with an iron scuffle on those ill weeds that make the garden-walks of life unsightly, when a sprinkle of Attic salt will wither them up. *Est ars etiam maledicendi*, says Scaliger, and truly it is a hard thing to say where the graceful gentleness of the lamb merges in downright sheepishness. We may conclude with worthy and wise Dr. Fuller, that "one may be a lamb in private wrongs, but in hearing general affronts to goodness they are asses which are not lions." — H. W.

GUVENER B. is a sensible man;
    He stays to his home an' looks arter his folks,
He draws his furrer ez straight ez he can,
    An' into nobody's tater-patch pokes; —
                But John P.
                Robinson he
    Sez he wunt vote fer Guvener B.

My! aint it terrible?   Wut shall we du?
    We can't never choose him, o' course, — thet 's
        flat;
Guess we shall hev to come round, (don't you?)
    An' go in fer thunder an' guns, an all that;
                Fer John P.
                Robinson he
    Sez he wunt vote fer Guvener B.

Gineral C. is a dreffle smart man:
    He 's ben on all sides thet give places or pelf;
But consistency still wuz a part of his plan, —
    He 's ben true to *one* party, — an' thet is him-
        self, —
                So John P.
                Robinson he
    Sez he shall vote fer Gineral C.

Gineral C. he goes in fer the war;
    He don't vally principle more 'n an old cud;
Wut did God make us raytional creeturs fer,
    But glory an' gunpowder, plunder an' blood?

So John P.
Robinson he
Sez he shall vote fer Gineral C.

We were gittin' on nicely up here to our village,
    With good old idees o' wut's right an' wut
        aint,
We kind o' thought Christ went agin war an' pil-
        lage,
    An' thet eppyletts wor n't the best mark of a
        saint ;
                But John P.
                Robinson he
        Sez this kind o' thing 's an exploded idee.

The side of our country must ollers be took,
    An' Presidunt Polk, you know, *he* is our coun-
        try,
An' the angel thet writes all our sins in a book
    Puts the *debit* to him, an' to us the *per contry* ;   ,
                An' John P.
                Robinson he
        Sez this is his view o' the thing to a T.

Parson Wilbur he calls all these argimunts lies ;
    Sez they 're nothin' on airth but jest *fee, faw,
        fum ;*
An' thet all this big talk of our destinies
    Is half on it ignorance an' t'other half
        rum ;

But John P.

Robinson he

Sez it aint no sech thing; an', of course, so
must we.

Parson Wilbur sez *he* never heerd in his life

Thet th' Apostles rigged out in their swaller-
tail coats

An' marched round in front of a drum an' a fife,

To git some on 'em office, an' some on 'em
votes,

But John P.

Robinson he

Sez they did n't know everythin' down in
Judee.

Wal, it 's a marcy we 've gut folks to tell us

The rights an' the wrongs o' these matters, I
vow ;

God sends country lawyers, an' other wise fellers,

To drive the world's team wen it gits in a
slough,

Fer John P.

Robinson he

Sez the world 'll go right, ef he hollers out
Gee.

[The attentive reader will doubtless have perceived
in the foregoing poem an allusion to that pernicious
sentiment, "Our country, right or wrong." It is an

abuse of language to call a certain portion of land, much more, certain personages elevated for the time being to high station, our country. I would not sever nor loosen a single one of those ties by which we are united to the spot of our birth, nor minish by a tittle the respect due to the Magistrate. I love our own Bay State too well to do the one, and as for the other, I have myself for nigh forty years exercised, however unworthily, the function of Justice of the Peace, having been called thereto by the unsolicited kindness of that most excellent man and upright patriot, Caleb Strong. *Patriæ fumus igne alieno luculentior* is best qualified with this, *Ubi libertas, ibi patria.* We are inhabitants of two worlds, and owe a double, but not a divided, allegiance. In virtue of our clay, this little ball of earth exacts a certain loyalty of us, while, in our capacity as spirits, we are admitted citizens of an invisible and holier fatherland. There is a patriotism of the soul whose claim absolves us from our other and terrene fealty. Our true country is that ideal realm which we represent to ourselves under the names of religion, duty, and the like. Our terrestrial organizations are but far-off approaches to so fair a model, and all they are verily traitors who resist not any attempt to divert them from this their original intendment. When, therefore, one would have us to fling up our caps and shout with the multitude, " *Our country, however bounded !* " he demands of us that we sacrifice the larger to the less, the higher to the lower, and that we yield to the imaginary claims of a few acres of soil our duty and privilege as liegemen of Truth. Our true country is bounded on the north and the south, on the east and the west, by Justice, and when she oversteps that invisible boundary-line by so much as a hair's-breadth, she ceases to be our mother, and chooses rather to be looked upon *quasi noverca.* That is a hard choice, when our earthly love of country calls upon us to tread one path and our duty points us to another. We must make as noble and becoming an election as did Penelope between Icarius and Ulysses. Veiling our faces, we must take silently the hand of Duty to follow her.

Shortly after the publication of the foregoing poem, there appeared some comments upon it in one of the public prints which seemed to call for some animadversion. I accordingly addressed to Mr. Buckingham, of the Boston Courier, the following letter : —

"JAALAM, November 4, 1847.

" To the Editor of the Courier :

" RESPECTED SIR, — Calling at the post-office this morning, our worthy and efficient postmaster offered for my perusal a paragraph in the Boston Morning Post of the 3d instant, wherein certain effusions of the pastoral muse are attributed to the pen of Mr. James Russell Lowell. For aught I know or can affirm to the contrary, this Mr. Lowell may be a very deserving person and a youth of parts (though I have seen verses of his which I could never rightly understand) ; and if he be such, he, I am certain, as well as I, would be free from any proclivity to appropriate to himself whatever of credit (or discredit) may honestly belong to another. I am confident, that, in penning these few lines, I am only forestalling a disclaimer from that young gentleman, whose silence hitherto, when rumor pointed to himward, has excited in my bosom mingled emotions of sorrow and surprise.   Well may my young parishioner, Mr. Biglow, exclaim with the poet,

' Sic vos non vobis,' etc.

though, in saying this, I would not convey the impression that he is a proficient in the Latin tongue, — the tongue, I might add, of a Horace and a Tully.

"Mr. B. does not employ his pen, I can safely say, for any lucre of worldly gain, or to be exalted by the carnal plaudits of men, *digito monstrari*, etc.   He does not wait upon Providence for mercies, and in his heart mean *merces*.   But I should esteem myself as verily deficient in my duty (who am his friend and in some unworthy sort his spiritual *fidus Achates*, etc.), if I did not step forward to claim for him whatever measure of applause might be assigned to him by the judicious.

"If this were a fitting occasion, I might venture here a brief dissertation touching the manner and kind of my young friend's poetry.   But I dubitate whether this abstruser sort of speculation (though enlivened by some apposite instances from Aristophanes) would sufficiently interest your oppidan readers. As regards their satirical tone, and their plainness of speech, I will only say, that, in my pastoral experience, I have found that the Arch-Enemy loves nothing better than to be treated as a religious, moral, and intellectual being, and that there is no *apage Sathanas!* so potent as ridicule.   But it is a kind of weapon that must have a button of good-nature on the point of it.

" The productions of Mr. B. have been stigmatized in some quarters as unpatriotic ; but I can vouch that he loves his native soil with that hearty, though discriminating, attachment which springs from an intimate social intercourse of many years' standing. In the ploughing season, no one has a deeper share in the well-being of the country than he. If Dean Swift were right in saying that he who makes two blades of grass grow where one grew before confers a greater benefit on the state than he who taketh a city, Mr. B. might exhibit a fairer claim to the Presidency then General Scott himself. I think that some of those disinterested lovers of the hard-handed democracy, whose fingers have never touched anything rougher than the dollars of our common country, would hesitate to compare palms with him. It would do your heart good, respected Sir, to see that young man mow. He cuts a cleaner and wider swarth than any in this town.

"But it is time for me to be at my Post. It is very clear that my young friend's shot has struck the lintel, for the Post is shaken (Amos ix. 1). The editor of that paper is a strenuous advocate of the Mexican war, and a colonel, as I am given to understand. I presume, that, being necessarily absent in Mexico, he has left his journal in some less judicious hands. At any rate, the Post has been too swift on this occasion. It could hardly have cited a more incontrovertible line from any poem than that which it has selected for animadversion, namely,—

'We kind o' thought Christ went agin war an' pillage.'

"If the Post maintains the converse of this proposition, it can hardly be considered as a safe guide-post for the moral and religious portions of its party, however many other excellent qualities of a post it may be blessed with. There is a sign in London on which is painted, 'The Green Man.' It would do very well as a portrait of any individual who would support so unscriptural a thesis. As regards the language of the line in question, I am bold to say that He who readeth the hearts of men will not account any dialect unseemly which conveys a sound and pious sentiment. I could wish that such sentiments were more common, however uncouthly expressed. Saint Ambrose affirms, that *veritas a quocunque* (why not, then, *quomodocunque?*) *dicatur, a spiritu sancto est.* Digest also this of Baxter: 'The plainest words are the most profitable oratory in the weightiest matters.'

"When the paragraph in question was shown to Mr. Biglow, the only part of it which seemed to give him any dissatisfaction was that which classed him with the Whig party. He says, that, if resolutions are a nourishing kind of diet, that party must be in a very hearty and flourishing condition ; for that they have quietly eaten more good ones of their own baking than he could have conceived to be possible without repletion. He has been for some years past (I regret to say) an ardent opponent of those sound doctrines of protective policy which form so prominent a portion of the creed of that party. I confess, that, in some discussions which I have had with him on this point in my study, he has displayed a vein of obstinacy which I had not hitherto detected in his composition. He is also (*horresco referens*) infected in no

small measure with the peculiar notions of a print
called the Liberator, whose heresies I take every
proper opportunity of combating, and of which, I
thank God, I have never read a single line.

"I did not see Mr. B.'s verses until they appeared
in print, and there *is* certainly one thing in them
which I consider highly improper. I allude to the
personal references to myself by name. To confer
notoriety on an humble individual who is laboring
quietly in his vocation, and who keeps his cloth as
free as he can from the dust of the political arena
(though *væ mihi si non evangelizavero*), is no doubt an
indecorum. The sentiments which he attributes to
me I will not deny to be mine. They were embodied,
though in a different form, in a discourse preached
upon the last day of public fasting, and were accept-
able to my entire people (of whatever political views),
except the postmaster, who dissented *ex officio*. I ob-
serve that you sometimes devote a portion of your
paper to a religious summary. I should be well
pleased to furnish a copy of my discourse for insertion
in this department of your instructive journal. By
omitting the advertisements, it might easily be got
within the limits of a single number, and I venture
to insure you the sale of some scores of copies in this
town. I will cheerfully render myself responsible
for ten. It might possibly be advantageous to issue
it as an *extra*. But perhaps you will not esteem it an
object, and I will not press it. My offer does not
spring from any weak desire of seeing my name in
print ; for I can enjoy this satisfaction at any time
by turning to the Triennial Catalogue of the Uni-
versity, where it also possesses that added emphasis

of Italics with which those of my calling are distinguished.

"I would simply add, that I continue to fit ingenuous youth for college, and that I have two spacious and airy sleeping apartments at this moment unoccupied. *Ingenuas didicisse,* etc. Terms, which vary according to the circumstances of the parents, may be known on application to me by letter, post paid. In all cases the lad will be expected to fetch his own towels. This rule, Mrs. W. desires me to add, has no exceptions.

"Respectfully, your obedient servant,

"HOMER WILBUR, A. M.

"P. S. Perhaps the last paragraph may look like an attempt to obtain the insertion of my circular gratuitously. If it should appear to you in that light, I desire that you would erase it, or charge for it at the usual rates, and deduct the amount from the proceeds in your hands from the sale of my discourse, when it shall be printed. My circular is much longer and more explicit, and will be forwarded without charge to any who may desire it. It has been very neatly executed on a letter sheet, by a very deserving printer, who attends upon my ministry, and is a creditable specimen of the typographic art. I have one hung over my mantelpiece in a neat frame, where it makes a beautiful and appropriate ornament, and balances the profile of Mrs. W., cut with her toes by the young lady born without arms.   H. W."

I have in the foregoing letter mentioned General Scott in connection with the Presidency, because I

have been given to understand that he has blown to
pieces and otherwise caused to be destroyed more
Mexicans than any other commander. His claim
would therefore be deservedly considered the strong-
est. Until accurate returns of the Mexican killed,
wounded, and maimed be obtained, it will be difficult
to settle these nice points of precedence. Should it
prove that any other officer has been more meritorious
and destructive than General S., and has thereby ren-
dered himself more worthy of the confidence and sup-
port of the conservative portion of our community, I
shall cheerfully insert his name, instead of that of
General S., in a future edition. It may be thought,
likewise, that General S. has invalidated his claims by
too much attention to the decencies of apparel, and
the habits belonging to a gentleman. These ab-
struser points of statesmanship are beyond my scope.
I wonder not that successful military achievement
should attract the admiration of the multitude.
Rather do I rejoice with wonder to behold how rap-
idly this sentiment is losing its hold upon the popular
mind. It is related of Thomas Warton, the second of
that honored name who held the office of Poetry Pro-
fessor at Oxford, that, when one wished to find him,
being absconded, as was his wont, in some obscure
alehouse, he was counselled to traverse the city with a
drum and fife, the sound of which inspiring music
would be sure to draw the Doctor from his retirement
into the street. We are all more or less bitten with
this martial insanity. *Nescio quâ dulcedine . . .
cunctos ducit.* I confess to some infection of that itch
myself. When I see a Brigadier-General maintain-
ing his insecure elevation in the saddle under the

severe fire of the training-field, and when I remember that some military enthusiasts, through haste, inexperience, or an over-desire to lend reality to those fictitious combats, will sometimes discharge their ramrods, I cannot but admire, while I deplore, the mistaken devotion of those heroic officers. *Semel insanivimus omnes.* I was myself, during the late war with Great Britain, chaplain of a regiment, which was fortunately never called to active military duty. I mention this circumstance with regret rather than pride. Had I been summoned to actual warfare, I trust that I might have been strengthened to bear myself after the manner of that reverend father in our New England Israel, Dr. Benjamin Colman, who, as we are told in Turell's life of him, when the vessel in which he had taken passage for England was attacked by a French privateer, "fought like a philosopher and a Christian, . . . and prayed all the while he charged and fired." As this note is already long, I shall not here enter upon a discussion of the question, whether Christians may lawfully be soldiers. I think it sufficiently evident, that, during the first two centuries of the Christian era, at least, the two professions were esteemed incompatible. Consult Jortin on this head. — H. W.]

No. IV.

[THE ingenious reader will at once understand that
no such speech as the following was ever *totidem verbis*
pronounced. But there are simpler and less guarded
wits, for the satisfying of which such an explanation
may be needful. For there are certain invisible lines,
which as Truth successively overpasses, she becomes
Untruth to one and another of us, as a large river,
flowing from one kingdom into another, sometimes
takes a new name, albeit the waters undergo no
change, how small soever. There is, moreover, a
truth of fiction more veracious than the truth of fact,
as that of the Poet, which represents to us things and
events as they ought to be, rather than servilely copies
them as they are imperfectly imaged in the crooked
and smoky glass of our mundane affairs. It is this
which makes the speech of Antonius, though originally
spoken in no wider a forum than the brain of Shak-
speare, more historically valuable than that other which
Appian has reported, by as much as the understand-
ing of the Englishman was more comprehensive than
that of the Alexandrian. Mr. Biglow, in the present
instance, has only made use of a license assumed by
all the historians of antiquity, who put into the

mouths of various characters such words as seem to
them most fitting to the occasion and to the speaker.
If it be objected that no such oration could ever have
been delivered, I answer, that there are few assem-
blages for speech-making which do not better deserve
the title of *Parliamentum Indoctorum* than did the
sixth Parliament of Henry the Fourth, and that men
still continue to have as much faith in the Oracle of
Fools as ever Pantagruel had.   Howell, in his letters,
recounts a merry tale of a certain ambassador of
Queen Elizabeth, who, having written two letters,
one to her Majesty and the other to his wife, directed
them at cross purposes, so that the Queen was be-
ducked and bedeared and requested to send a change
of hose, and the wife was beprincessed and otherwise
unwontedly besuperlatived, till the one feared for the
wits of her ambassador, the other for those of her
husband.   In like manner it may be presumed that
our speaker has misdirected some of his thoughts,
and given to the whole theatre what he would have
wished to confide only to a select auditory at the back
of the curtain.   For it is seldom that we can get any
frank utterance from men, who address, for the most
part, a Buncombe either in this world or the next.   As
for their audiences, it may be truly said of our people,
that they enjoy one political institution in common with
the ancient Athenians : I mean a certain profitless kind
of *ostracism*, wherewith, nevertheless, they seem hith-
erto well enough content.   For in Presidential elec-
tions, and other affairs of the sort, whereas I observe
that the *oysters* fall to the lot of comparatively few,
the *shells* (such as the privileges of voting as they are
told to do by the *ostrivori* aforesaid, and of huzzaing

at public meetings) are very liberally distributed among the people, as being their prescriptive and quite sufficient portion.

The occasion of the speech is supposed to be Mr. Palfrey's refusal to vote for the Whig candidate for the Speakership. — H. W.]

No? Hez he? He haint, though? Wut? Voted
    agin him?
Ef the bird of our country could ketch him,
    she 'd skin him;
I seem 's though I see her, with wrath in each
    quill
Like a chancery lawyer, afilin' her bill,
An' grindin' her talents ez sharp ez all nater,
To pounce like a writ on the back o' the traiter.
Forgive me, my friends, ef I seem to be het,
But a crisis like this must with vigor be met;
Wen an Arnold the star-spangled banner be-
    stains,
Holl Fourth o' Julys seem to bile in my veins.

Who ever 'd ha' thought sech a pisonous rig
Would be run by a chap thet wuz chose fer a
    Wig?
"We knowed wut his principles wuz 'fore we
    sent him?"
Wut wuz ther in them from this vote to pervent
    him?
A marciful Providunce fashioned us holler
O' purpose thet we might our principles swaller;

It can hold any quantity on 'em, the belly can,
An' bring 'em up ready fer use like the pelican,
Or more like the kangaroo, who (wich is stranger)
Puts her family into her pouch wen there's
    danger.
Aint principle precious? then, who's goin' to
    use it
Wen there's resk o' some chap's gittin' up to
    abuse it?
I can't tell the wy on 't, but nothin' is *so* sure
Ez thet principle kind o' gits spiled by ex-
    posure ; [1]
A man thet lets all sorts o' folks git a sight on 't
Ough' to hev it all took right away, every mite
    on 't ;
Ef he can't keep it all to himself wen it's
    wise to,
He aint one it's fit to trust nothin' so nice to.

Besides, ther's a wonderful power in latitude
To shift a man's morril relations an' attitude ;

[1] The speaker is of a different mind from Tully, who, in
his recently discovered tractate *De Republicâ*, tells us, —
*Nec vero habere virtutem satis est, quasi artem aliquam, nisi
utare,* and from our Milton, who says, "I cannot praise a
fugitive and cloistered virtue, unexercised and unbreathed,
that never sallies out and sees her adversary, but slinks out
of the race where that immortal garland is to be run for, *not
without dust and heat*." — *Areop.* He had taken the words
out of the Roman's mouth, without knowing it, and might
well exclaim with Austin (if a saint's name may stand spon-
sor for a curse), *Pereant qui ante nos nostra dixerint !* —
H. W.

Some flossifers think thet a fakkilty 's granted
The minnit it 's proved to be thoroughly wanted,
Thet a change o' demand makes a change o' con-
        dition,
An' thet everythin' 's nothin' except by position ;
Ez fer instance, thet rubber-trees fust begun
        bearin'
Wen p'litickle conshunces come into wearin', —
Thet the fears of a monkey, whose holt chanced
        to fail,
Drawed the vertibry out to a prehensile tail ;
So, wen one 's chose to Congriss, ez soon ez he 's
        in it,
A collar grows right round his neck in a minnit,
An' sartin it is thet a man cannot be strict
In bein' himself, wen he gits to the Deestrict,
Fer a coat thet sets wal here in ole Massachu-
        setts,
Wen it gits on to Washinton, somehow askew
        sets.

Resolves, do you say, o' the Springfield Conven-
        tion ?
Thet 's percisely the pint I was goin' to men-
        tion ;
Resolves air a thing we most gen'ally keep ill,
They 're a cheap kind o' dust fer the eyes 'o the
        people ;   •
A parcel o' delligits jest git together
An' chat fer a spell o' the crops an' the weather,

Then, comin' to order, they squabble awile,
An' let off the speeches they 're ferful 'll spile ;
Then — Resolve, — Thet we wunt hev an inch
  o' slave territory ;
Thet President Polk's holl perceedins air very
  tory ;
Thet the war 's a damned war, an' them thet
  enlist in it
Should hev a cravat with a dreffle tight twist
  in it ;
Thet the war is a war fer the spreadin' o' slav-
  ery ;
Thet our army desarves our best thanks fer their
  bravery ;
Thet we 're the original friends o' the nation,
All the rest air a paltry an' base fabrication ;
Thet we highly respect Messrs. A, B, an' C,
An' ez deeply despise Messrs. E, F, an' G.
In this way they go to the eend o' the chapter,
An' then they bust out in a kind of a raptur
About their own vartoo, an' folk's stone-blind-
  ness
To the men thet 'ould actilly do 'em a kind-
  ness, —
The American eagle, the Pilgrims thet landed,
Till on ole Plymouth Rock they git finally
  stranded ;
Wal, the people they listen and say, " Thet 's
  the ticket ;
Ez fer Mexico, t'aint no great glory to lick it,

But 't would be a darned shame to go pullin' o'
    triggers
To extend the aree of abusin' the niggers."
So they march in percessions, an' git up hooraws,
An' tramp thru the mud fer the good o' the
    cause,
An' think they 're a kind o' fulfillin' the prophe-
    cies,
Wen they 're on'y jest changin' the holders of
    offices!
Ware A sot afore, B is comf'tably seated,
One humbug 's victor'ous an' t'other defeated.
Each honnable doughface gits jest wut he axes,
An' the people — their annooal soft sodder an'
    taxes.

Now, to keep unimpaired all these glorious feeturs
Thet characterize morril and reasonin' creeturs,
Thet give every paytriot all he can cram,
Thet oust the untrustworthy Presidunt Flam,
And stick honest Presidunt Sham in his place
To the manifest gain o' the holl human race,
An' to some indervidgewals on 't in partickler,
Who love Public Opinion an' know how to tickle
    her, —
I say thet a party with great aims like these
Must stick jest ez close ez a hive full o' bees.

I 'm willin' a man should go tollable strong
Agin wrong in the abstract, fer thet kind o'
    wrong

Is ollers unpop'lar an' never gits pitied,
Because it's a crime no one never committed;
But he mus'n't be hard on partickler sins,
Coz then he 'll be kickin' the people's own shins.
On'y look at the Demmercrats, see wut they 've
      done
Jest simply by stickin' together like fun;
They 've sucked us right into a mis'able war
Thet no one on airth aint responsible for;
They 've run us a hundred cool millions in debt,
(An' fer Demmercrat Horners ther's good plums
      left yet;)
They talk agin tayriffs, but act fer a high one,
An' so coax all parties to build up their Zion;
To the people they 're ollers ez slick ez molas-
      ses,
An' butter their bread on both sides with The
      Masses,
Half o' whom they 've persuaded, by way of a
      joke,
Thet Washinton's mantelpiece fell upon Polk.

Now all o' these blessins the Wigs might enjoy,
Ef they 'd gumption enough the right means to
      imploy; [1]
Fer the silver spoon born in Dermocracy's mouth
Is a kind of a scringe thet they hev to the South;

---

[1] That was a pithy saying of Persius, and fits our politi-
cians without a wrinkle, *Magister artis, ingeniique largitor
venter.* — H. W.

Their masters can cuss 'em an' kick 'em an' wale
    'em,
An' they notice it less 'an the ass did to Balaam;
In this way they screw into second-rate offices
Wich the slave-holder thinks 'ould substract too
    much off his ease;
The file-leaders, I mean, du, fer they, by their
    wiles,
Unlike the old viper, grow fat on their files.
Wal, the Wigs hev been tryin' to grab all this
    prey frum 'em
An' to hook this nice spoon o' good fortin' away
    frum 'em,
An' they might ha' succeeded ez likely ez not,
In lickin' the Demmercrats all round the lot,
Ef it war n't thet, wile all faithful Wigs were
    their knees on,
Some stuffy old codger would holler out, —
    " Treason !
You must keep a sharp eye on a dog thet hez bit
    you once,
An' *I* aint agoin' to cheat my constitoounts," —
Wen every fool knows thet a man represents
Not the fellers thet sent him, but them on the
    fence, —
Impartially ready to jump either side
An' make the fust use of a turn o' the tide, —
The waiters on Providunce here in the city,
Who compose wut they call a State Centerl Com-
    mitty.

Constitoounts air hendy to help a man in,
But arterwards don't weigh the heft of a pin.
Wy, the people can't all live on Uncle Sam's pus,
So they 've nothin' to du with 't fer better or
    wus ;
It 's the folks thet air kind o' brought up to de-
    pend on 't
Thet hev any consarn in 't, and thet is the end
    on 't.

Now here wuz New England ahevin' the honor
Of a chance at the Speakership showered upon
    her ; —
Do you say, " She don't want no more Speak-
    ers, but fewer ;
She 's hed plenty o' them, wut she wants is a
    doer " ?
Fer the matter o' thet, it 's notorous in town
Thet her own representatives du her quite brown.
But thet 's nothin' to du with it ; wut right hed
    Palfrey
To mix himself up with fanatical small fry ?
War n't we gittin' on prime with our hot an' cold
    blowin'
Acondemnin' the war wilst we kep' it agoin' ?
We 'd assumed with gret skill a commandin'
    position,
On this side or thet, no one could n't tell wich
    one,
So, wutever side wipped, we 'd a chance at the
    plunder

An' could sue fer infringin' our paytented thun-
    der ;
We were ready to vote fer whoever wuz eligible,
Ef on all pints at issoo he 'd stay unintelligible.
Wal, sposin' we hed to gulp down our perfes-
    sions,
We were ready to come out next mornin' with
    fresh ones ;
Besides, ef we did, 't was our business alone,
Fer could n't we du wut we would with our own ?
An' ef a man can, wen pervisions hev riz so,
Eat up his own words, it 's a marcy it is so.

Wy, these chaps frum the North, with back-
    bones to 'em, darn 'em,
'Ould be wuth more 'an Gennle Tom Thumb is
    to Barnum ;
Ther 's enough thet to office on this very plan
    grow,
By exhibitin' how very small a man can grow ;
But an M. C. frum here ollers hastens to state he
Belongs to the order called invertebraty,
Wence some gret filologists judge primy fashy
Thet M. C. is M. T. by paronomashy ;
An' these few exceptions air *loosus naytury*
Folks 'ould put down their quarters to stare at
    like fury.

It 's no use to open the door o' success,
Ef a member can bolt so fer nothin' or less ;

Wy, all o' them grand constitootional pillers
Our four fathers fetched with 'em over the bil-
    lers,
Them pillers the people so soundly hev slept on,
Wile to slav'ry, invasion, an' debt they were
    swept on,
Wile our Destiny higher an' higher kep' mount-
    in',
(Though I guess folks 'll stare wen she hends
    her account in,)
Ef members in this way go kickin' agin 'em,
They wunt hav so much ez a feather left in 'em.

An', ez fer this Palfrey,[1] we thought wen we 'd
    gut him in,
He 'd go kindly in wutever harness we put him in ;
Supposin' we *did* know thet he wuz a peace man ?
Doos he think he can be Uncle Samwell's police-
    man,
An' wen Sam gits tipsy an' kicks up a riot,
Lead him off to the lockup to snooze till he 's
    quiet ?
Wy, the war is a war thet true paytriots can bear,
    ef
It leads to the fat promised land of a tayriff ;
We don't go an' fight it, nor aint to be driv on,
Nor Demmercrats nuther, thet hev wut to live
    on ;

---

[1] There is truth yet in this of Juvenal, —
      " Dat veniam corvis, vexat censura columbas."

Ef it aint jest the thing thet 's well pleasin' to
     God,
It makes us thought highly on elsewhere abroad ;
The Rooshian black eagle looks blue in his eerie
An' shakes both his heads wen he hears o' Mon-
     teery ;
In the Tower Victory sets, all of a fluster,
An' reads, with locked doors, how we won Cherry
     Buster ;
An' old Philip Lewis — thet come an' kep' school
     here
Fer the mere sake o' scorin' his ryalist ruler
On the tenderest part of our kings *in futuro* —
Hides his crown underneath an old shut in his
     bureau,
Breaks off in his brags to a suckle o' merry kings,
How he often hed hided young native Amerri-
     kins,
An', turnin' quite faint in the midst of his fooler-
     ies,
Sneaks down stairs to bolt the front door o' the
     Tooleries.[1]

[1] Jortin is willing to allow of other miracles besides those recorded in Holy Writ, and why not of other prophecies ? It is granting too much to Satan to suppose him, as divers of the learned have done, the inspirer of the ancient oracles. Wiser, I esteem it, to give chance the credit of the successful ones. What is said here of Louis Philippe was verified in some of its minute particulars within a few months' time. Enough to have made the fortune of Delphi or Hammon, and no thanks to Beelzebub neither ! That of Seneca in Medea will suit here : —

You say, " We 'd ha' scared 'em by growin' in
    peace
A plaguy sight more then by bobberies like
    these " ?
Who is it dares say thet " our naytional eagle
Wun't much longer be classed with the birds
    thet air regal,
Coz theirn be hooked beaks, an' she, arter this
    slaughter,
'll bring back a bill ten times longer 'n she ough'
    to " ?
Wut 's your name?   Come, I see ye, you up-
    country feller,
You 've put me out severil times with your
    beller ;
Out with it!   Wut?   Biglow?   I say nothin'
    furder ;
Thet feller would like nothin' better 'n a murder ;
He 's a traiter, blasphemer, an' wut ruther worse
    is,
He puts all his ath'ism in dreffle bad verses ;
Socity aint safe till sech monsters air out on it,
Refer to the Post, ef you hev the least doubt
    on it ;

> " Rapida fortuna ac levis,
> Præcepsque regno eripuit, exsilio dedit."

Let us allow, even to richly deserved misfortune, our com-
miseration, and be not over-hasty meanwhile in our censure
of the French people, left for the first time to govern them-
selves, remembering that wise sentence of Æschylus, —

᾿Άπας δὲ τραχὺς ὅστις ἂν νέον κρατῇ.

H. W.

Wy, he goes agin war, agin indirect taxes,
Agin sellin' wild lands 'cept to settlers with axes,
Agin holdin' o' slaves, though he knows it 's the
    corner
Our libbaty rests on, the mis'able scorner!
In short, he would wholly upset with his ravages
All thet keeps us above the brute critters an'
    savages,
An' pitch into all kinds o' briles an' confusions
The holl of our civilized, free institutions ;
He writes fer thet rather unsafe print, the
    Courier,
An' likely ez not hez a squintin' to Foorier ;
I 'll be ——, thet is, I mean I 'll be blest,
Ef I hark to a word frum so noted a pest ;
I shan't talk with *him*, my religion 's too fervent.
Good mornin', my friends, I 'm your most humble
    servant.

[Into the question, whether the ability to express ourselves in articulate language has been productive of more good or evil, I shall not here enter at large. The two faculties of speech and of speech-making are wholly diverse in their natures. By the first we make ourselves intelligible, by the last unintelligible, to our fellows. It has not seldom occurred to me (noting how in our national legislature everything runs to talk, as lettuces, if the season or the soil be unpropitious, shoot up lankly to seed, instead of forming handsome heads) that Babel was the first Congress, the earliest mill erected for the manufacture of gabble.   In these days, what with Town Meetings, School Committees, Boards (lumber) of one kind and another, Congresses, Parliaments, Diets, Indian Councils, Palavers, and the like, there is scarce a village which has not its factories of this description driven by (milk-and-) water power.   I cannot conceive the confusion of tongues to have been the curse of Babel, since I esteem my ignorance of other languages as a kind of Martello-tower, in which I am safe from the furious bombardments of foreign garrulity.   For this reason I have ever preferred the study of the dead languages, those primitive formations being Ararats upon whose silent peaks I sit secure and watch this new deluge without fear, though it rain figures (*simulacra*, semblances) of speech forty days and nights together, as it not uncommonly happens.   Thus is my coat, as it were, without buttons by which any but a vernacular wild bore can seize me.   Is it not possible that the Shakers may intend to convey a quiet reproof and hint, in fastening their outer garments with hooks and eyes ?

This reflection concerning Babel, which I find in no Commentary, was first thrown upon my mind when an excellent deacon of my congregation (being infected with the Second Advent delusion) assured me that he had received a first instalment of the gift of tongues as a small earnest of larger possessions in the like kind to follow.   For, of a truth, I could not reconcile it with my ideas of the Divine justice and mercy that the single wall which protected people of other languages from the incursions of this otherwise well-meaning propagandist should be broken down.

In reading Congressional debates, I have fancied,

that, after the subsidence of those painful buzzings in
the brain which result from such exercises, I detected
a slender residuum of valuable information. I made
the discovery that *nothing* takes longer in the saying
than anything else, for, as *ex nihilo nihil fit,* so from
one polypus *nothing* any number of similar ones may
be produced. I would recommend to the attention
of *vivâ voce* debaters and controversialists the admira-
ble example of the monk Copres, who, in the fourth
century, stood for half an hour in the midst of a great
fire, and thereby silenced a Manichæan antagonist
who had less of the salamander in him. As for those
who quarrel in print, I have no concern with them
here, since the eyelids are a divinely granted shield
against all such. Moreover, I have observed in many
modern books that the printed portion is becoming
gradually smaller, and the number of blank or fly-
leaves (as they are called) greater. Should this for-
tunate tendency of literature continue, books will
grow more valuable from year to year, and the whole
Serbonian bog yield to the advances of firm arable
land.

I have wondered, in the Representatives' Chamber
of our own Commonwealth, to mark how little im-
pression seemed to be produced by that emblematic
fish suspended over the heads of the members. Our
wiser ancestors, no doubt, hung it there as being the
animal which the Pythagoreans reverenced for its
silence, and which certainly in that particular does
not so well merit the epithet *cold-blooded,* by which
naturalists distinguish it, as certain bipeds, afflicted
with ditch-water on the brain, who take occasion to
tap themselves in Fanueil Halls, meeting-houses, and
other places of public resort.—H. W.]

No. V.

THE DEBATE IN THE SENNIT.

SOT TO A NUSRY RHYME.

[THE incident which gave rise to the debate satirized in the following verses was the unsuccessful attempt of Drayton and Sayres to give freedom to seventy men and women, fellow-beings and fellow-Christians. Had Tripoli, instead of Washington, been the scene of this undertaking, the unhappy leaders in it would have been as secure of the theoretic as they now are of the practical part of martyrdom. I question whether the Dey of Tripoli is blessed with a District Attorney so benighted as ours at the seat of government. Very fitly is he named Key, who would allow himself to be made the instrument of locking the door of hope against sufferers in such a cause. Not all the waters of the ocean can cleanse the vile smutch of the jailer's fingers from off that little Key. *Ahenea clavis*, a brazen Key indeed!

Mr. Calhoun, who is made the chief speaker in this burlesque, seems to think that the light of the nineteenth century is to be put out as soon as he tinkles his little cow-bell curfew. Whenever slavery is touched, he sets up his scarecrow of dissolving the Union. This may do for the North, but I should conjecture that something more than a pumpkin-lantern is required to scare manifest and irretrievable Destiny out of her path. Mr. Calhoun cannot let go the apron-string of the Past. The Past is a good nurse, but we must be weaned from her sooner or later, even though, like Plotinus, we should run home from school to ask the breast, after we are tolerably well-grown youths. It will not do for us to hide our faces in her lap, whenever the strange Future holds out her arms and asks us to come to her.

But we are all alike. We have all heard it said, often enough, that little boys must not play with fire ; and yet, if the matches be taken away from us and put out of reach upon the shelf, we must needs get into our little corner, and scowl and stamp and threaten the dire revenge of going to bed without our supper. The world shall stop till we get our dangerous plaything again. Dame Earth, meanwhile, who has more than enough household matters to mind, goes bustling hither and thither as a hiss or a sputter tells her that this or that kettle of hers is boiling over, and before bedtime we are glad to eat our porridge cold, and gulp down our dignity along with it.

Mr. Calhoun has somehow acquired the name of a great statesman, and, if it be great statesmanship to put lance in rest and run a tilt at the Spirit of the Age with the certainty of being next moment hurled neck and heels into the dust amid universal laughter, he deserves the title. He is the Sir Kay of our modern chivalry. He should remember the old Scandinavian mythus. Thor was the strongest of gods, but he could not wrestle with Time, nor so

much as lift up a fold of the great snake which knit
the universe together ; and when he smote the
Earth, though with his terrible mallet, it was but as
if a leaf had fallen.   Yet all the while it semed to
Thor that he had only been wrestling with an old
woman, striving to lift a cat, and striking a stupid
giant on the head.

And in old times, doubtless, the giants *were* stupid,
and there was no better sport for the Sir Launcelots
and Sir Gawains than to go about cutting off their
great blundering heads with enchanted swords.   But
things have wonderfully changed.   It is the giants,
nowadays, that have the science and the intelli-
gence, while the chivalrous Don Quixotes of Conser-
vatism still cumber themselves with the clumsy armor
of a bygone age.   On whirls the restless globe through
unsounded time, with its cities and its silences, its
births and funerals, half light, half shade, but never
wholly dark, and sure to swing round into the happy
morning at last.   With an involuntary smile, one
sees Mr. Calhoun letting slip his pack-thread cable
with a crooked pin at the end of it to anchor South
Carolina upon the bank and shoal of the Past. — H.
W.]

TO MR. BUCKENAM.

MR. EDITER, As i wuz kinder prunin
round, in a little nussry sot out a year or 2
a go, the Dbait in the sennit cum inter my
mine An so i took & Sot it to wut I call a
nussry rime.   I hev made sum onnable
Gentlemun speak that dident speak in a

Kind uv Poetikul lie sense the seeson is dreffle backerd up This way

    ewers as ushul

        HOSEA BIGLOW.

" HERE we stan' on the Constitution, by thun-
        der !
It 's a fact o' wich ther 's bushils o' proofs ;
Fer how could we trample on 't so, I wonder,
    Ef 't wor n't thet it 's ollers under our hoofs ? "
        Sez John C. Calhoun, sez he ;
            " Human rights haint no more
            Right to come on this floor,
        No more 'n the man in the moon," sez he.

" The North haint no kind o' bisness with
        nothin',
    An' you 've no idee how much bother it saves ;
We aint none riled by their frettin' an' frothin',
    We 're *used* to layin' the string on our slaves,"
        Sez John C. Calhoun, sez he ; —
            Sez Mister Foote,
            " I should like to shoot
        The holl gang, by the gret horn spoon ! "
        sez he.

" Freedom's Keystone is Slavery, thet ther 's no
        doubt on,
    It 's sutthin' thet 's — wha' d' ye call it? —
        divine, —

An' the slaves thet we ollers *make* the most out
    on
  Air them north o' Mason an' Dixon's line,"
    Sez John C. Calhoun, sez he ; —
      " Fer all thet," sez Mangum,
      " 'T would be better to hang 'em,
    An' so get red on 'em soon," sez he.

" The mass ough' to labor an' we lay on soffies,
  Thet 's the reason I want to spread Freedom's
    aree ;
It puts all the cunninest on us in office,
  An' reelises our Maker's orig'nal idee,"
    Sez John C. Calhoun, sez he ; —
      " Thet 's ez plain," sez Cass,
      " Ez thet some one 's an ass,
    It 's ez clear ez the sun is at noon," sez he.

" Now don't go to say I 'm the friend of oppres-
    sion,
  But keep all your spare breath fer coolin' your
    broth ;
Fer I ollers hev strove (at least thet 's my im-
    pression)
  To make cussed free with the rights o' the
    North."
    Sez John C. Calhoun, sez he ; —
      " Yes." sez Davis o' Miss.,
      " The perfection o' bliss
    Is in skinnin' thet same old coon," sez he.

" Slavery 's a thing thet depends on complexion,
    It 's God's law thet fetters on black skins don't
        chafe ;
Ef brains wuz to settle it (horrid reflection !)
    Wich of our onnable body 'd be safe ? "
        Sez John C. Calhoun, sez he ; —
        Sez Mister Hannegan,
        Afore he began agin, `
        " Thet exception is quite oppertoon," sez he.

" Gen'nle Cass, Sir, you need n't be twitchin'
        your collar,
    Your merit 's quite clear by the dut on your
        knees,
At the North we don't make no distinctions o'
        color ;
    You can all take a lick at our shoes wen you
        please,"
        Sez John C. Calhoun, sez he ; —
        Sez Mister Jarnagin,
        " They wunt hev to larn agin,
        They all on 'em know the old toon," sez he.

" The slavery question aint no ways bewilderin'.
    North an' South hev one int'rest, it 's plain to
        a glance,
No'thern men, like us patriarchs, don't sell their
        childrin,
    But they du sell themselves, ef they git a good
        chance,"

Sez John C. Calhoun, sez he ; —
    Sez Atherton here,
    " This is gittin' severe,
I wish I could dive like a loon," sez he.

" It 'll break up the Union, this talk about free-
        dom,
    An' your fact'ry gals (soon ez we split) 'll make
        head,
An' gittin' some Miss chief or other to lead 'em,
    'll go to work raisin' promiscoous Ned,"
        Sez John C. Calhoun, sez he ; —
        " Yes, the North," sez Colquitt,
        " Ef we Southerners all quit,
    Would go down like a busted balloon," sez
        he.

" Jest look wut is doin', wut annyky's brewin'
    In the beautiful clime o' the olive an' vine,
All the wise aristoxy is tumblin' to ruin,
    An' the sankylots drorin' an' drinkin their
        wine,"
        Sez John C. Calhoun, sez he, —
        " Yes," sez Johnson, " in France
        They 're beginnin' to dance
    Beelzebub's own rigadoon," sez he.

" The South 's safe enough, it don't feel a mite
        skeery,
    Our slaves in their darkness an' dut air tu blest

Not tu welcome with proud hallylugers the cry
  Wen our eagle kicks yourn from the naytional
      nest,"
    Sez John C. Calhoun, sez he ; —
    " O," sez Westcott o' Florida,
    " Wut treason is horrider
    Then our priv'leges tryin' to proon ? " sez he.

" It 's 'coz they 're so happy, thet wen crazy sar-
      pints
  Stick their nose in our bizness, we git so
      darned riled
We think it 's our dooty to give pooty sharp hints,
  Thet the last crumb of Edin on airth shan't
      be spiled
    Sez John C. Calhoun, sez he ; —
    " Ah," sez Dixon H. Lewis,
    " It perfectly true is
    Thet slavery 's airth's grettest boon," sez he.

[It was said of old time, that riches have wings ;
and, though this be not applicable in a literal strict-
ness to the wealth of our patriarchal brethren of the
South, yet it is clear that their possessions have legs,
and an unaccountable propensity for using them in a
northerly direction.   I marvel that the grand jury
of Washington did not find a true bill against the
North Star for aiding and abetting Drayton and
Sayres.   It would have been quite of a piece with
the intelligence displayed by the South on other
questions connected with slavery.   I think that no

ship of state was ever freighted with a more veritable
Jonah than this same domestic institution of ours.
Mephistopheles himself could not feign so bitterly, so
satirically sad a sight as this of three millions of
human beings crushed beyond help or hope by this
one mighty argument, — *Our fathers knew no better!*
Nevertheless, it is the unavoidable destiny of Jonahs
to be cast overboard sooner or later. Or shall we try
the experiment of hiding our Jonah in a safe place,
that none may lay hands on him to make jetsam of
him ?   Let us, then, with equal forethought and wis-
dom, lash ourselves to the anchor, and await, in pious
confidence, the certain result. Perhaps our suspicious
passenger is no Jonah after all, being black. For it
is well known that a superintending Providence made
a kind of sandwich of Ham and his descendants, to
be devoured by the Caucasian race.

In God's name, let all, who hear nearer and nearer
the hungry moan of the storm and the growl of the
breakers, speak out ! But, alas ! we have no right
to interfere. If a man pluck an apple of mine, he
shall be in danger of the justice ; but if he steal my
brother, I must be silent. Who says this ? Our
Constitution, consecrated by the callous suetude of
sixty years, and grasped in triumphant argument in
the left hand of him whose right hand clutches the
clotted slave-whip. Justice, venerable with the un-
dethronable majesty of countless æons, says, —
SPEAK ! The Past, wise with the sorrows and desola-
tions of ages, from amid her shattered fanes and
wolf-housing palaces, echoes, — SPEAK !   Nature,
through her thousand trumpets of freedom, her stars,
her sunrises, her seas, her winds, her cataracts, her

mountains blue with cloudy pines, blows jubilant
encouragement, and cries,— SPEAK ! From the
soul's trembling abysses the still, small voice not
vaguely murmurs, — SPEAK ! But, alas ! the Consti-
tution and the Honorable Mr. Bagowind, M. C., say,
— BE DUMB !

It occurs to me to suggest, as a topic of inquiry in
this connection, whether, on that momentous occasion
when the goats and the sheep shall be parted, the
Constitution and the Honorable Mr. Bagowind, M.
C., will be expected to take their places on the left
as our hircine vicars.

Quid sum miser tunc dicturus?
Quem patronum rogaturus ?

There is a point where toleration sinks into sheer
baseness and poltroonery. The toleration of the
worst leads us to look on what is barely better as
good enough, and to worship what is only moderately
good. Woe to that man, or that nation, to whom
mediocrity has become an ideal !

Has our experiment of self-government succeeded,
if it barely manage to *rub and go?* Here, now, is a
piece of barbarism which Christ and the nineteenth
century say shall cease, and which Messrs. Smith,
Brown, and others say shall *not* cease. I would by
no means deny the eminent respectability of these
gentlemen, but I confess, that, in such a wrestling-
match, I cannot help having my fears for them.

Discite justitiam, moniti, et non temnere divos.

H. W.]

THE PIOUS EDITOR'S CREED.

[AT the special instance of Mr. Biglow, I preface the following satire with an extract from a sermon preached during the past summer, from Ezekiel xxxiv. 2 : "Son of man, prophesy against the shepherds of Israel." Since the Sabbath on which this discourse was delivered, the editor of the "Jaalam Independent Blunderbuss" has unaccountably absented himself from our house of worship.

"I know of no so responsible position as that of the public journalist. The editor of our day bears the same relation to his time that the clerk bore to the age before the invention of printing. Indeed, the position which he holds is that which the clergyman should hold even now. But the clergyman chooses to walk off to the extreme edge of the world, and to throw such seed as he has clear over into that darkness which he calls the Next Life. As if *next* did not mean *nearest*, and as if any life were nearer than that immediately present one which boils and eddies all around him at the caucus, the ratification meeting, and the polls! Who taught him to exhort men to prepare for eternity, as for some future era of which the present forms no integral part? The furrow which Time is even now turning runs through the

Everlasting, and in that must he plant, or nowhere.
Yet he would fain believe and teach that we are
going to have more of eternity than we have now.
This *going* of his is like that of the auctioneer, on
which *gone* follows before we have made up our
minds to bid, — in which manner, not three months
back, I lost an excellent copy of Chappelow on Job.
So it has come to pass that the preacher, instead of
being a living force, has faded into an emblematic
figure at christenings, weddings, and funerals. Or,
if he exercise any other function, it is as keeper and
feeder of certain theologic dogmas, which, when oc-
casion offers, he unkennels with a *staboy!* "to bark
and bite as 't is their nature to," whence that re-
proach of *odium theologicum* has arisen.

"Meanwhile, see what a pulpit the editor mounts
daily, sometimes with a congregation of fifty thou-
sand within reach of his voice, and never so much as
a nodder, even, among them! And from what a
Bible can he choose his text, — a Bible which needs
no translation, and which no priestcraft can shut and
clasp from the laity, — the open volume of the world,
upon which, with a pen of sunshine or destroying fire,
the inspired Present is even now writing the annals
of God! Methinks the editor who should understand
his calling, and be equal thereto, would truly deserve
that title of ποιμὴν λαῶν, which Homer bestows upon
princes. He would be the Moses of our nineteenth
century, and whereas the old Sinai, silent now, is but
a common mountain stared at by the elegant tourist
and crawled over by the hammering geologist, he
must find his tables of the new law here among fac-
tories and cities in this Wilderness of Sin (Numbers

xxxiii. 12) called Progress of Civilization, and be the captain of our Exodus into the Canaan of a truer social order.

"Nevertheless, our editor will not come so far within even the shadow of Sinai as Mahomet did, but chooses rather to construe Moses by Joe Smith. He takes up the crook, not that the sheep may be fed, but that he may never want a warm woollen suit and a joint of mutton.

Immemor, O, fidei, pecorumque oblite tuorum!

For which reason I would derive the name *editor* not so much from *edo*, to publish, as from *edo*, to eat, that being the peculiar profession to which he esteems himself called. He blows up the flames of political discord for no other occasion than that he may thereby handily boil his own pot. I believe there are two thousand of these mutton-loving shepherds in the United States, and of these, how many have even the dimmest perception of their immense power, and the duties consequent thereon? Here and there, haply, one. Nine hundred and ninety-nine labor to impress upon the people the great principles of *Tweedledum*, and other nine hundred and ninety-nine preach with equal earnestness the gospel according to *Tweedledee.*"
— H. W.]

> I DU believe in Freedom's cause,
>   Ez fur away ez Paris is;
> I love to see her stick her claws
>   In them infarnal Pharisees;
> It's wal enough agin a king
>   To dror resolves an' triggers, —

But libbaty 's a kind o' thing
   Thet don't agree with niggers.

I du believe the people want
   A tax on teas an' coffees,
Thet nothin' aint extravygunt, —
   Purvidin' I 'm in office ;
Fer I hev loved my country sence
   My eye-teeth filled their sockets,
An' Uncle Sam I reverence,
   Partic'larly his pockets.

I du believe in *any* plan
   O' levyin' the taxes,
Ez long ez, like a lumberman,
   I git jest wut I axes :
I go free-trade thru thick an' thin,
   Because it kind o' rouses
The folks to vote, — an' keeps us in
   Our quiet custom-houses.

I du believe it 's wise an' good
   To sen' out furrin missions,
Thet is, on sartin understood
   An' orthydox conditions ; —
I mean nine thousan' dolls. per ann.,
   Nine thousan' more fer outfit,
An' me to recommend a man
   The place 'ould jest about fit.

I du believe in special ways
    O' prayin' an' convartin';
The bread comes back in many days,
    An' buttered, tu, fer sartin; —
I mean in preyin' till one busts
    On wut the party chooses,
An' in convartin' public trusts
    To very privit uses.

I du believe hard coin the stuff
    Fer 'lectioneers to spout on;
The people 's ollers soft enough
    To make hard money out on;
Dear Uncle Sam pervides fer his,
    An' gives a good-sized junk to all, —
I don't care *how* hard money is,
    Ez long ez mine 's paid punctooal.

I du believe with all my soul
    In the gret Press's freedom,
To pint the people to the goal
    An' in the traces lead 'em;
Palsied the arm thet forges yokes
    At my fat contracts squintin',
An' withered be the nose thet pokes
    Inter the gov'ment printin'!

I du believe thet I should give
    Wut 's his'n unto Cæsar,

Fer it 's by him I move an' live,
    Frum him my bread an' cheese air ;
I du believe thet all o' me
    Doth bear his souperscription, —
Will, conscience, honor, honesty,
    An' things o' thet description.

I du believe in prayer an' praise
    To him thet hez the grantin'
O' jobs, — in every thin' thet pays,
    But most of all in CANTIN' ;
This doth my cup with marcies fill,
    This lays all thought o' sin to rest, —
I *don't* believe in princerple,
    But, O, I *du* in interest.

I du believe in bein' this
    Or thet, ez it may happen
One way or t' other hendiest is
    To ketch the people nappin' ;
It aint by princerples nor men
    My preudunt course is steadied, —
I scent wich pays the best, an' then
    Go into it baldheaded.

I du believe thet holdin' slaves
    Comes nat'ral tu a Presidunt,
Let 'lone the rowdedow it saves
    To hev a wal-broke precedunt ;

Fer any office, small or gret,
    I could n't ax with no face,
Without I 'd ben, thru dry an' wet,
    Th' unrizzest kind o' doughface.

I du believe wutever trash
    'll keep the people in blindness, —
Thet we the Mexicuns can thrash
    Right inter brotherly kindness,
Thet bombshells, grape, an' powder 'n' ball
    Air good-will's strongest magnets,
Thet peace, to make it stick at all,
    Must be druv in with bagnets.

In short, I firmly du believe
    In Humbug generally,
Fer it 's a thing thet I perceive
    To hev a solid vally ;
This heth my faithful shepherd ben,
    In pasturs sweet heth led me,
An' this 'll keep the people green
    To feed ez they hev fed me.

[I subjoin here another passage from my before-
mentioned discourse.

" Wonderful, to him that has eyes to see it rightly,
is the newspaper. To me, for example, sitting on
the critical front bench of the pit, in my study here
in Jaalam, the advent of my weekly journal is as
that of a strolling theatre, or rather of a puppet-

show, on whose stage, narrow as it is, the tragedy, comedy, and farce of life are played in little. Behold the whole huge earth sent to me hebdomadally in a brown-paper wrapper !

"Hither, to my obscure corner, by wind or steam, on horse-back, or dromedary-back, in the pouch of the Indian runner, or clicking over the magnetic wires, troop all the famous performers from the four quarters of the globe. Looked at from a point of criticism, tiny puppets they seem all, as the editor sets up his booth upon my desk and officiates as showman. Now I can truly see how little and transitory is life. The earth appears almost as a drop of vinegar, on which the solar microscope of the imagination must be brought to bear in order to make out anything distinctly. That animalcule there, in the pea-jacket, is Louis Philippe, just landed on the coast of England. That other, in the gray surtout and cocked hat, is Napoleon Bonaparte Smith, assuring France that she need apprehend no interference from him in the present alarming juncture. At that spot, where you seem to see a speck of something in motion, is an immense mass-meeting. Look sharper, and you will see a mite brandishing his mandibles in an excited manner. That is the great Mr. Soandso, defining his position amid tumultuous and irrepressible cheers. That infinitesimal creature, upon whom some score of others, as minute as he, are gazing in open-mouthed admiration, is a famous philosopher, expounding to a select audience their capacity for the Infinite. That scarce discernible pufflet of smoke and dust is a revolution. That speck there is a reformer, just arranging the lever with which he is to move the world. And lo, there creeps forward the shadow of a skeleton that blows one breath between its grinning teeth, and all our distinguished actors are whisked off the slippery stage into the dark Beyond.

" Yes, the little show-box has its solemner suggestions. Now and then we catch a glimpse of a grim old man, who lays down a scythe and hour-glass in the corner while he shifts the scenes. There, too, in the dim back-ground, a weird shape is ever delving. Sometimes he leans upon his mattock, and gazes, as a coach whirls by, bearing the newly married on their wedding jaunt, or glances carelessly at a babe brought home from christening. Suddenly (for the scene grows larger and larger as we look) a bony hand snatches back a performer in the midst of his part, and him, whom yesterday two infinities (past and future) would not suffice, a handful of dust is enough to cover and silence forever. Nay, we see the same fleshless fingers opening to clutch the showman himself, and guess, not without a shudder, that they are lying in wait for spectator also.

" Think of it : for three dollars a year I buy a season-ticket to this great Globe Theatre, for which God would write the dramas (only that we like farces, spectacles, and the tragedies of Apollyon better), whose scene-shifter is Time, and whose curtain is rung down by Death.

" Such thoughts will occur to me sometimes as I am tearing off the wrapper of my newspaper. Then suddenly that otherwise too often vacant sheet becomes invested for me with a strange kind of awe. Look ! deaths and marriages, notices of inventions, discoveries, and books, lists of promotions, of killed, wounded, and missing, news of fires, accidents, of sudden wealth and as sudden poverty ; — I hold in my hand the ends of myriad invisible electric conductors, along which tremble the joys, sorrows, wrongs, triumphs, hopes, and despairs of as many men and women everywhere. So that upon that mood of mind which seems to isolate me from mankind as a spectator of their puppet-pranks, another supervenes, in which I feel that I, too, unknown and unheard of, am yet of some import to my fellows. For, through my newspaper here, do not families take pains to send me, an entire stranger, news of a death among them ? Are not here two who would have me know of their marriage ? And, strangest of all, is not this singular person anxious to have me informed that he has received a fresh supply of Dimitry Bruisgins ? But to none of us does the Present (even if for a moment discerned as such) continue miraculous. We glance carelessly at the sunrise, and get used to Orion and the Pleiades. The wonder wears off, and to-morrow this sheet, in which a vision was let down to me from Heaven, shall be the wrappage to a bar of soap or the platter for a beggar's broken victuals." — H. W.]

No. VII.

A LETTER

FROM A CANDIDATE FOR THE PRESIDENCY IN AN-
SWER TO SUTTIN QUESTIONS PROPOSED BY MR.
HOSEA BIGLOW, INCLOSED IN A NOTE FROM MR.
BIGLOW TO S. H. GAY, ESQ., EDITOR OF THE
NATIONAL ANTI-SLAVERY STANDARD.

[CURIOSITY may be said to be the quality which preëminently distinguishes and segregates man from the lower animals. As we trace the scale of animated nature downward, we find this faculty of the mind (as it may truly be called) diminished in the savage, and quite extinct in the brute. The first object which civilized man proposes to himself I take to be the finding out whatsoever he can concerning his neighbors. *Nihil humanum a me alienum puto;* I am curious even about John Smith. The desire next in strength to this (an opposite pole, indeed, of the same magnet) is that of communicating intelligence.

Men in general may be divided into the inquisitive and the communicative. To the first class belong Peeping Toms, eaves-droppers, navel-contemplating Brahmins, metaphysicians, travellers, Empedocleses, spies, the various societies for promoting Rhinothism, Columbuses, Yankees, discoverers, and men of science, who present themselves to the mind as so many marks of interrogation wandering up and down the world, or sitting in studies and laboratories. The second class I should again subdivide into four. In the first subdivision I would rank those who have an itch to tell us about themselves, — as keepers of diaries, insignificant persons generally, Montaignes, Horace Walpoles, autobiographers, poets. The second includes those who are anxious to impart information concerning other people, — as historians, barbers, and such. To the third belong those who labor to give us intelligence about nothing at all, — as novelists, political orators, the large majority of authors, preachers, lecturers, and the like. In the fourth come those who are communicative from motives of public benevolence, — as finders of mares'-nests and bringers of ill news. Each of us two-legged fowls without feathers embraces all these subdivisions in himself to a greater or less degree, for none of us so much as lays an egg, or incubates a chalk one, but straightway the whole barn-yard shall know it by our cackle or our cluck. *Omnibus hoc vitium est.* There are different grades in all these classes. One will turn his telescope toward a back-yard, another toward Uranus ; one will tell you that he dined with Smith, another that he supped with Plato. In one particular, all men may be considered as belonging to the first grand division, inasmuch as they all seem equally desirous of discovering the mote in their neighbor's eye.

To one or another of these species every human being may safely be referred. I think it beyond a peradventure that Jonah prosecuted some inquiries into the digestive apparatus of whales, and that Noah sealed up a letter in an empty bottle, that news in regard to him might not be wanting in case of the worst. They had else been super or subter human. I conceive, also, that, as there are certain persons who continually peep and pry at the key-hole of that mysterious door through which, sooner or later, we all make our exits, so there are doubtless ghosts fidgeting and fretting on the other side of it, because they have no means of conveying back to the world the scraps of news they have picked up. For there is an answer ready somewhere to every question, the great law of *give and take* runs through all nature, and if we see a hook, we may be sure that an eye is waiting for it. I read in every face I meet a standing advertisement of information wanted in regard to A. B., or that the friends of C. D. can hear of him by application to such a one.

It was to gratify the two great passions of asking and answering that epistolary correspondence was first invented. Letters (for by this usurped title epistles are now commonly known) are of several kinds. First, there are those which are not letters at all, — as letters patent, letters dimissory, letters inclosing bills, letters of administration, Pliny's letters, letters of diplomacy, of Cato, of Mentor, of Lords Lyttelton, Chesterfield, and Orrery, of Jacob Behmen, Seneca (whom St. Jerome includes in his list of sacred writers), letters from abroad, from sons in college to their fathers, letters of marque, and letters generally, which are in no wise letters of mark. Second, are real letters, such as those of Gray, Cowper, Walpole, Howel, Lamb, the first letters from children (printed in staggering capitals), Letters from New York, letters of credit, and others, inter-

esting for the sake of the writer or the thing written.
I have read also letters from Europe by a gentle-
man named Pinto, containing some curious gossip,
and which I hope to see collected for the benefit of
the curious. There are, besides, letters addressed
to posterity, — as epitaphs, for example, written for
their own monuments by monarchs, whereby we have
lately become possessed of the names of several great
conquerors and kings of kings, hitherto unheard of
and still unpronounceable, but valuable to the stu-
dent of the entirely dark ages. The letter which St.
Peter sent to King Pepin in the year of grace 755 I
would place in a class by itself, as also the letters of
candidates, concerning which I shall dilate more fully
in a note at the end of the following poem. At pres-
ent, *sat prata biberunt.* Only, concerning the shape
of letters, they are all either square or oblong, to
which general figures circular letters and round-
robins also conform themselves. — H. W.]

DEER SIR its gut to be the fashun now to
rite letters to the candid 8s and i wus chose
at a publick Meetin in Jaalam to du wut
wus nessary fur that town. i writ to 271
ginerals and gut ansers to 209. tha air
called candid 8s but I don't see nothin can-
did about em. this here 1 wich I send wus
thought satty's factory. I dunno as it's
ushle to print Poscrips, but as all the ansers
I got hed the saim, I sposed it wus best.
times has gretly changed. Formerly to

knock a man into a cocked hat wus to use
him up, but now it only gives him a chance
fur the cheef madgustracy. — H. B.

DEAR SIR, — You wish to know my notions
   On sartin pints thet rile the land;
There's nothin' thet my nature so shuns
   Ez bein' mum or underhand;
I'm a straight-spoken kind o' creetur
   Thet blurts right out wut's in his head,
An' ef I've one pecooler feetur,
   It is a nose thet wunt be led.

So, to begin at the beginnin',
   An' come direcly to the pint,
I think the country's underpinnin'
   Is some consid'ble out o' jint;
I aint agoin' to try your patience
   By tellin' who done this or thet,
I don't make no insinooations,
   I jest let on I smell a rat.

Thet is, I mean, it seems to me so,
   But, ef the public think I'm wrong,
I wunt deny but wut I be so, —
   An,' fact, it don't smell very strong;
My mind's tu fair to lose its balance
   An' say wich party hez most sense;
There may be folks o' greater talence
   Thet can't set stiddier on the fence.

I 'm an eclectic ; ez to choosin'
   Twixt this an' thet, I 'm plaguy lawth ;
I leave a side thet looks like losin',
   But (wile there 's doubt) I stick to both ;
I stan' upon the Constitution,
   Ez preudunt statesmun say, who 've planned
A way to git the most profusion
   O' chances ez to *ware* they 'll stand.

Ez fer the war, I go agin it, —
   I mean to say I kind o' du, —
Thet is, I mean thet, bein' in it,
   The best way wuz to fight it thru ;
Not but wut abstract war is horrid,
   I sign to thet with all my heart, —
But civlyzation *doos* git forrid
   Sometimes upon a powder-cart.

About thet darned Proviso matter
   I never hed a grain o' doubt,
Nor I aint one my sense to scatter
   So 's no one could n't pick it out ;
My love fer North an' South is equil,
   So I 'll jest answer plump an' frank,
No matter wut may be the sequil, —
   Yes, Sir, I *am* agin a Bank.

Ez to the answerin' o' questions,
   I 'm an off ox at bein' druv,
Though I aint one thet ary test shuns
   'll give our folks a helpin' shove ;

Kind o' promiscoous I go it
  Fer the holl country, an' the ground
I take, ez nigh ez I can show it,
  Is pooty gen'ally all round.

I don't appruve o' givin' pledges;
  You 'd ough' to leave a feller free
An' not go knockin' out the wedges
  To ketch his fingers in the tree;
Pledges air awfle breachy cattle
  Thet preudunt farmers don't turn out, —
Ez long 'z the people git their rattle,
  Wut is there fer 'm to grout about?

Ez to the slaves, there 's no confusion
  In *my* idees consarnin' them, —
I think they air an Institution,
  A sort of — yes, jest so, ahem:
Do *I* own any? Of my merit
  On thet pint you yourself may jedge;
All is, I never drink no sperit,
  Nor I haint never signed no pledge.

Ez to my principles, I glory
  In hevin' nothin' o' the sort;
I aint a Wig, I aint a Tory,
  I 'm jest a candidate, in short;
Thet 's fair an' square an' parpendicler
  But, ef the Public cares a fig
To hev me an' thin' in particler,
  Wy, I 'm a kind o' peri-wig.

P. S.

Ez we 're a sort o' privateerin',
　　O' course, you know, it 's sheer an' sheer,
An' there is sutthin' wuth your hearin'
　　I 'll mention in *your* privit ear ;
Ef you git *me* inside the White House,
　　Your head with ile I 'll kin' o' 'nint
By gittin' *you* inside the Light-house
　　Down to the eend 'o Jaalam Pint.

An' ez the North hez took to brustlin'
　　At bein' scrouged frum off the roost,
I 'll tell ye wut 'll save all tusslin'
　　An' give our side a harnsome boost,—
Tell 'em thet on the Slavery question
　　I 'm RIGHT, although to speak I 'm lawth.
This gives you a safe pint to rest on,
　　An' leaves me frontin' South by North.

[And now of epistles candidatial, which are of two
kinds, — namely, letters of acceptance, and letters
definitive of position. Our republic, on the eve of
an election, may safely enough be called a republic
of letters. Epistolary composition becomes then an
epidemic, which seizes one candidate after another,
not seldom cutting short the thread of political life.
It has come to such a pass, that a party dreads less
the attacks of its opponents than a letter from its
candidate. *Litera scripta manet*, and it will go hard

if something bad cannot be made of it. General Harrison, it is well understood, was surrounded, during his candidacy, with the *cordon sanitaire* of a vigilance committee.   No prisoner in Spielberg was ever more cautiously deprived of writing materials. The soot was scraped carefully from the chimney-places ; outposts of expert rifle-shooters rendered it sure death for any goose (who came clad in feathers) to approach within a certain limited distance of North Bend ; and all domestic fowls about the premises were reduced to the condition of Plato's original man. By these precautions the General was saved. *Parva componere magnis*, I remember, that, when party-spirit once ran high among my people, upon occasion of the choice of a new deacon, I, having my preferences, yet not caring too openly to express them, made use of an innocent fraud to bring about the result which I deemed most desirable. My stratagem was no other than the throwing a copy of the Complete Letter-Writer in the way of the candidate whom I wished to defeat. He caught the infection, and addressed a short note to his constituents, in which the opposite party detected so many and so grave improprieties (he had modelled it upon the letter of a young lady accepting a proposal of marriage), that he not only lost his election, but, falling under a suspicion of Sabellianism and I know not what (the widow Endive assured me that he was a Paralipomenon, to her certain knowledge), was forced to leave the town. Thus it is that the letter killeth.

The object which candidates propose to themselves in writing is to convey no meaning at all. And here is a quite unsuspected pitfall into which they successively plunge headlong. For it is precisely in such cryptographies that mankind are prone to seek for and find a wonderful amount and variety of significance. *Omne ignotum pro mirifico.* How do we admire at the antique world striving to crack those oracular nuts from Delphi, Hammon, and elsewhere, in only one of which can I so much as surmise that any kernel had ever lodged ; that, namely, wherein Apollo confessed that he was mortal. One Didymus is, moreover, related to have written six thousand books on the single subject of grammar, a topic rendered only more tenebrific by the labors of his successors, and which seems still to possess an attraction for authors in proportion as they can make nothing of it. A singular loadstone for theologians, also, is the Beast in the Apocalypse, whereof, in the course of my studies, I have noted two hundred and three several interpretations, each lethiferal to all the rest. *Non nostrum est tantas componere lites,* yet I have myself ventured upon a two hundred and fourth, which I embodied in a discourse preached on occasion of the demise of the late usurper, Napoleon Bonaparte, and which quieted, in a large measure, the minds of my people. It is true that my views on this important point were ardently controverted by Mr. Shearjashub Holden, the then preceptor of our academy, and in other particulars a very deserving and sensible young man, though possessing a somewhat limited knowledge of the Greek tongue. But his heresy struck down no deep root, and, he having been lately removed by the hand of Providence, I had the satisfaction of reaffirming my cherished sentiments in a sermon preached upon the Lord's day immediately succeeding his funeral. This might seem like taking an unfair advantage, did I not add that he had made provision in his last will (being celibate) for the publication of a posthumous tractate in support of his own dangerous opinions.

I know of nothing in our modern times which approaches so nearly to the ancient oracle as the letter of a Presidential candidate. Now, among the Greeks, the eating of beans was strictly forbidden to all such as had it in mind to consult those expert amphibologists, and this same prohibition on the part of Pythagoras to his disciples is understood to imply an abstinence from politics, beans having been used as ballots. That other explication, *quod videlicet sensus eo cibo obtundi existimaret*, though supported *pugnis et calcibus* by many of the learned, and not wanting the countenance of Cicero, is confuted by the larger experience of New England. On the whole, I think it safer to apply here the rule of interpretation which now generally obtains in regard to antique cosmogonies, myths, fables, proverbial expressions, and knotty points generally, which is, to find a common-sense meaning, and then select whatever can be imagined the most opposite thereto. In this way we arrive at the conclusion, that the Greeks objected to the questioning of candidates. And very properly, if, as I conceive, the chief point be not to discover what a person in that position is, or what he will do, but whether he can be elected. *Vos exemplaria Græca nocturna versate manu, versate diurna.*

But, since an imitation of the Greeks in this particular (the asking of questions being one chief privilege of freemen) is hardly to be hoped for, and our

candidates will answer, whether they are questioned
or not, I would recommend that these ante-election-
ary dialogues should be carried on by symbols, as
were the diplomatic correspondences of the Scythians
and Macrobii, or confined to the language of signs,
like the famous interview of Panurge and Goatsnose.
A candidate might then convey a suitable reply to all
committees of inquiry by closing one eye, or by pre-
senting them with a phial of Egyptian darkness to be
speculated upon by their respective constituencies.
These answers would be susceptible of whatever re-
trospective construction the exigencies of the politi-
cal campaign might seem to demand, and the candi-
date could take his position on either side of the fence
with entire consistency. Or, if letters must be writ-
ten, profitable use might be made of the Dighton
rock hieroglyphic or the cuneiform script, every fresh
decipherer of which is enabled to educe a different
meaning, whereby a sculptured stone or two supplies
us, and will probably continue to supply posterity,
with a very vast and various body of authentic his-
tory. For even the briefest epistle in the ordinary
chirography is dangerous. There is scarce any style
so compressed that superfluous words may not be
detected in it. A severe critic might curtail that
famous brevity of Cæsar's by two thirds, drawing his
pen through the supererogatory *veni* and *vidi*. Per-
haps, after all, the surest footing of hope is to be
found in the rapidly increasing tendency to demand
less and less of qualification in candidates. Already
have statesmanship, experience, and the possession
(nay, the profession, even) of principles been rejected
as superfluous, and may not the patriot reasonably

hope that the ability to write will follow ?   At present, there may be death in pot-hooks as well as pots, the loop of a letter may suffice for a bow-string, and all the dreadful heresies of Anti-slavery may lurk in a flourish. — H. W.]

A SECOND LETTER FROM B. SAWIN, ESQ.

[IN the following epistle, we behold Mr. Sawin returning, a *miles emeritus*, to the bosom of his family. *Quantum mutatus!* The good Father of us all had doubtless intrusted to the keeping of this child of his certain faculties of a constructive kind. He had put in him a share of that vital force, the nicest economy of every minute atom of which is necessary to the perfect development of Humanity. He had given him a brain and heart, and so had equipped his soul with the two strong wings of knowledge and love, whereby it can mount to hang its nest under the eaves of heaven. And this child, so dowered, he had intrusted to the keeping of his vicar, the State. How stands the account of that stewardship? The State, or Society (call her by what name you will), had taken no manner of thought of him till she saw him swept out into the street, the pitiful leavings of last night's debauch, with cigar-ends, lemon-parings, tobacco-quids, slops, vile stenches, and the whole loathsome next-morning of the bar-room, — an own child of the Almighty God! I remember him as he was brought to be christened, a ruddy, rugged babe; and now there he wallows, reeking, seething, — the dead corpse, not of a man, but of a soul, — a putrefying lump, horrible for the life that is in it. Comes the wind of heaven, that good Samaritan, and parts the hair upon his forehead, nor is too nice to kiss those parched, cracked lips ; the morning opens upon him her eyes full of pitying sunshine, the sky yearns down to him, — and there he lies fermenting. O sleep ! let me not profane thy holy name by calling that stertorous unconsciousness a slumber ! By and by comes along the State, God's vicar. Does she say, " My poor, forlorn foster-child ! Behold here a force which I will make dig and plant and build for me ? " Not so, but, " Here is a recruit ready-made to my hand, a piece of destroying energy lying unprofitably idle." So she claps an ugly gray suit on him, puts a musket in his grasp, and sends him off, with Gubernatorial and other godspeeds, to do duty as a destroyer.

I made one of the crowd at the last Mechanics' Fair, and, with the rest, stood gazing in wonder at a perfect machine, with its soul of fire, its boiler-heart that sent the hot blood pulsing along the iron arteries, and its thews of steel. And while I was admiring the adaptation of means to end, the harmonious involutions of contrivance, and the never-bewildered complexity, I saw a grimed and greasy fellow, the imperious engine's lackey and drudge, whose sole office was to let fall, at intervals, a drop or two of oil upon a certain joint. Then my soul said within me, See there a piece of mechanism to which that other you marvel at is but as the rude first effort of a child, — a force which not merely suffices to set a few wheels in motion, but which can send an impulse all through the infinite future, — a contrivance, not for turning

out pins, or stitching button-holes, but for making
Hamlets and Lears. And yet this thing of iron shall
be housed, waited on, guarded from rust and dust,
and it shall be a crime but so much as to scratch it
with a pin ; while the other, with its fire of God in it,
shall be buffeted hither and thither, and finally sent
carefully a thousand miles to be the target for a
Mexican cannon-ball. Unthrifty Mother State ! My
heart burned within me for pity and indignation, and
I renewed this covenant with my own soul, — *In aliis
mansuetus ero, at, in blasphemiis contra Christum non
ita.* — H. W.]

I spose you wonder ware I be ; I can't tell, fer
          the soul o' me,
Exacly ware I be myself, — meanin' by thet the
          holl o' me.
Wen I left hum, I hed two legs, an' they worn't
          bad ones neither,
(The scaliest trick they ever played wuz bringin'
          on me hither,)
Now one on 'em 's I dunno ware ; — they thought
          I wuz adyin',
An' sawed it off because they said 't wuz kin' o'
          mortifyin' ;
I 'm willin' to believe it wuz, an' yit I don't see,
          nuther,
Wy one should take to feelin' cheap a minnit
          sooner 'n t' other,
Sence both wuz equilly to blame ; but things is ez
          they be ;

It took on so they took it off, an' thet's enough
 fer me :
There's one good thing, though, to be said about
 my wooden new one, —
The liquor can't git into it ez 't used to in the
 true one ;
So it saves drink ; an' then, besides, a feller
 could n't beg
A gretter blessin' then to hev one ollers sober
 peg ;
It's true a chap's in want o' two fer follerin' a
 drum,
But all the march I 'm up to now is jest to King-
 dom Come.

I 've lost one eye, but thet's a loss it's easy to
 supply
Out o' the glory thet I 've gut, fer thet is all my
 eye ;
An' one is big enough, I guess, by diligently
 usin' it,
To see all I shall ever git by way o' pay fer
 losin' it ;
Off'cers, I notice, who git paid fer all our thumps
 an' kickins,
Du wal by keepin' single eyes arter the fattest
 pickins ;
So, ez the eye's put fairly out, I 'll larn to go
 without it,
An' not allow *myself* to be no gret put out about
 it.

Now, le' me see, thet is n't all; I used, 'fore
    leavin' Jaalam,
To count things on my finger-eends, but sutthin'
    seems to ail 'em :
Ware 's my left hand? O, darn it, yes, I recollect
    wut 's come on 't;
I haint no left arm but my right, an' thet 's gut
    jest a thumb on 't;
It aint so hendy ez it wuz to cal'late a sum
    on 't.
I 've hed some ribs broke, — six (I b'lieve), —
    I haint kep' no account on 'em ;
Wen pensions git to be the talk, I 'll settle the
    amount on 'em.
An' now I 'm speakin' about ribs, it kin' o' brings
    to mind
One thet I could n't never break, — the one I
    lef' behind ;
Ef you should see her, jest clear out the spout o'
    your invention
An' pour the longest sweetnin' in about an an-
    nooal pension.
An' kin' o' hint (in case, you know, the critter
    should refuse to be
Consoled) I aint so 'xpensive now to keep ez wut
    I used to be ;
There 's one arm less, ditto one eye, an' then the
    leg thet 's wooden
Can be took off an' sot away wenever ther' s a
    puddin'.

I spose you think I 'm comin' back ez opperlunt
    ez thunder,
With shiploads o' gold images an' varus sorts o'
    plunder ;
Wal, 'fore I vullinteered, I thought this country
    wuz a sort o'
Canaan, a regl'ar Promised Land flowin' with
    rum an' water,
Ware propaty growed up like time, without no
    cultivation,
An' gold wuz dug ez taters be among our Yankee
    nation,
Ware nateral advantages were pufficly amazin',
Ware every rock there wuz about with precious
    stuns wuz blazin',
Ware mill-sites filled the country up ez thick ez
    you could cram 'em,
An' desput rivers run about abeggin' folks to
    dam 'em ;
Then there were meetinhouses, tu, chockful o'
    gold an' silver
Thet you could take, an' no one could n't hand
    ye in no bill fer ; —
Thet 's wut I thought afore I went, thet 's wut
    them fellers told us
Thet stayed to hum an' speechified an' to the
    buzzards sold us ;
I thought thet gold mines could be gut cheaper
    than china asters,
An' see myself acomin' back like sixty Jacob
    Astors ;

But sech idees soon melted down an' did n't
    leave a grease-spot ;
I vow my holl sheer o' the spiles would n't come
    nigh a V spot ;
Although, most anywares we 've ben, you need
    n't break no locks,
Nor run no kin' o' risks, to fill your pocket full
    o' rocks.
I guess I mentioned in my last some o' the
    nateral feeturs
O' this all-fiered buggy hole in th' way o' awfle
    creeturs,
But I fergut to name (new things to speak on so
    abounded)
How one day you 'll most die o' thust, an' 'fore
    the next git drownded.
The clymit seems to me jest like a teapot made
    o' pewter
Our Prudence hed, thet would n't pour (all she
    could du) to suit her ;
Fust place the leaves 'ould choke the spout, so 's
    not a drop 'ould dreen out,
Then Prude 'ould tip an' tip an' tip, till the holl
    kit bust clean out,
The kiver-hinge-pin bein' lost, tea-leaves an' tea
    an' kiver
'ould all come down *kerswosh !* ez though the
    dam broke in a river.
Jest so 't is here ; holl months there aint a day
    o' rainy weather,

An' jest ez th' officers 'ould be alayin' heads to-
    gether
Ez t' how they 'd mix their drink at sech a mil-
    ingtary deepot, —
'T 'ould pour ez though the lid wuz off the ever-
    lastin' teapot.
The cons'quence is, thet I shall take, wen I 'm
    allowed to leave here,
One piece o' propaty along, — an' thet 's the
    shakin' fever ;
It 's reggilar employment, though, an' thet aint
    thought to harm one,
Nor 't aint so tiresome ez it wuz with t' other leg
    an' arm on ;
An' it 's a consolation, tu, although it doos n't
    pay,
To hev it said you 're some gret shakes in any
    kin' of way.
'T worn't very long, I tell ye wut, I thought o'
    fortin-makin', —
One day a reg'lar shiver-de-freeze, an' next ez
    good ez bakin', —
One day abrilin' in the sand, then smoth'rin' in
    the mashes, —
Git up all sound, be put to bed a mess o' hacks
    an' smashes.
But then, thinks I, at any rate there 's glory to
    be hed, —
Thet 's an investment, arter all, thet may n't
    turn out so bad ;

But somehow, wen we 'd fit an' licked, I ollers
    found the thanks
Gut kin' o' lodged afore they come ez low down
    ez the ranks ;
The Gin'rals gut the biggest sheer, the Cunnles
    next an' so on, —
We never gut a blasted mite o' glory ez I know
    on,
An' spose we hed, I wonder how you 're goin' to
    contrive its
Division so 's to give a piece to twenty thousand
    privits ;
Ef you should multiply by ten the portion o' the
    brav'st one,
You would n't git more 'n half enough to speak
    of on a grave-stun ;
We git the licks, — we 're jest the grist thet 's
    put into War's hoppers ;
Leftenants is the lowest grade thet helps pick up
    the coppers.
It may suit folks thet go agin a body with a soul
    in 't,
An' aint contented with a hide without a bagnet
    hole in 't ;
But glory is a kin' o' thing *I* shan't pursue no
    furder,
Coz thet 's the off'cers parquisite, — yourn 's on'y
    jest the murder.

Wal, arter I gin glory up, thinks I at least
    there 's one

Thing in the bills we aint hed yit, an' thet's the
        GLORIOUS FUN ;
Ef once we git to Mexico, we fairly may persume
        we
All day an' night shall revel in the halls o' Mon-
        tezumy.
I 'll tell ye wut *my* revels wuz, an' see how you
        would like 'em ;
We never gut inside the hall : the nighest ever
        I come
Wuz stan'in' sentry in the sun (an', fact, it *seemed*
        a cent'ry)
A ketchin' smells o' biled an' roast thet come out
        thru the entry,
An' hearin', ez I sweltered thru my passes an'
        repasses,
A rat-tat-too o' knives an' forks, a clinkty-clink
        o' glasses :
I can't tell off the bill o' fare the Gin'rals hed
        inside ;
All I know is, thet out o' doors a pair o' soles
        wuz fried,
An' not a hunderd miles away frum ware this
        child wuz posted,
A Massachusetts citizen wuz baked an' biled an'
        roasted ;
The on'y thing like revellin' thet ever come to
        me
Wuz bein' routed out o' sleep by thet darned re-
        velee.

They say the quarrel 's settled now ; fer my part
      I 've some doubt on 't,
'T 'll take more fish-skin than folks think to take
      the rile clean out on 't ;
At any rate, I 'm so used up I can't do no more
      fightin,
The on'y chance thet 's left to me is politics or
      writin' ;
Now, ez the people 's gut to hev a milingtary
      man,
An' I aint nothin' else jest now, I 've hit upon a
      plan ;
The can'idatin' line, you know, 'ould suit me to
      a T,
An' ef I lose, 't wunt hurt my ears to lodge an-
      other flea ;
So I 'll set up ez can'idate fer any kin' o' office,
(I mean fer any thet includes good easy-cheers
      an soffies ;
Fer ez to runnin' fer a place ware work 's the
      time o' day,
You know thet s' wut I never did, — except the
      other way ;)
Ef it 's the Presidential cheer fer wich I 'd better
      run,
Wut two legs anywares about could keep up with
      my one ?
There aint no kin' o' quality in can'idates, it 's
      said,
So useful ez a wooden leg, — except a wooden
      head :

There 's nothin' aint so poppylar — (wy, it 's a
    parfect sin
To think wut Mexico hez paid fer Santy Anny's
    pin ;) —
Then I haint gut no principles, an', sence I wuz
    knee-high,
I never *did* hev any gret, ez you can testify ;
I 'm a decided peace-man, tu, an' go agin the
    war, —
Fer now the holl on 't 's gone an' past, wut is
    there to go *for ?*
Ef, wile you 're 'lectioneerin' round, some curus
    chaps should beg
To know my views o' state affairs, jest answer
    WOODEN LEG !
Ef they aint settisfied with thet, an' kin' o' pry
    an' doubt
An' ax fer sutthin' deffynit, jest say ONE EYE
    PUT OUT !
Thet kin' o' talk I guess you 'll find 'll answer
    to a charm,
An wen you 're druv tu nigh the wall, hol' up my
    missin' arm ;
Ef they should nose round fer a pledge, put on a
    vartoous look
An' tell 'em thet 's percisely wut I never gin nor
    — took !

Then you can call me " Timbertoes," — thet 's
    wut the people likes ;

Sutthin' combinin' morril truth with phrases sech
    ez strikes ;
Some say the people 's fond o' this, or thet, or
    wut you please, —
I tell ye wut the people want is jest correct
    idees ;
"Old Timbertoes," you see, 's a creed it 's safe
    to be quite bold on,
There 's nothin' in 't the other side can any ways
    git hold on ;
It 's a good tangible idee, a sutthin' to embody
Thet valooable class o' men who look thru bran-
    dy toddy ;
It gives a Party Platform, tu, jest level with the
    mind
Of all right-thinkin', honest folks thet mean to
    go it blind ;
Then there air other good hooraws to dror on ez
    you need 'em,
Sech ez the ONE-EYED SLARTERER, the BLOODY
    BIRDOFREDUM ;
Them 's wut takes hold o' folks thet think, ez
    well ez o' the masses,
An' makes you sartin o' the aid o' good men of
    all classes.

There 's one thing I 'm in doubt about, in order
    to be Presidunt,
It 's absolutely ne'ssary to be a Southern residunt ;
The Constitution settles thet, an' also thet a feller

Must own a nigger o' some sort, jet black, or
      brown, or yeller.
Now I haint no objections agin particklar climes,
Nor agin ownin' anythin' (except the truth some-
      times),
But, ez I haint no capital, up there among ye,
      may be,
You might raise funds enough fer me to buy a
      low-priced baby.

An' then, to suit the No'thern folks, who feel
      obleeged to say
They hate an' cuss the very thing they vote fer
      every day,
Say you 're assured I go full butt fer Libbaty's
      diffusion
An' made the purchis on'y jest to spite the In-
      stitootion ; —
But, golly! there 's the currier's hoss upon the
      pavement pawin' !
I 'll be more 'xplicit in my next.
              Yourn,
                BIRDOFREDOM SAWIN.

[We have now a tolerably fair chance of estimat-
ing how the balance-sheet stands between our re-
turned volunteer and glory. Supposing the entries
to be set down on both sides of the account in frac-
tional parts of one hundred, we shall arrive at some-
thing like the following result : —

Cr. B. Sawin, Esq., in account with (Blank) Glory. Dr.

By loss of one leg . . 20	To one 675th three cheers	
" do. one arm . 15	in Faneuil Hall . . 30	
" do. four fingers . 5	" do. do. on	
" do. one eye . 10	occasion of presentation	
" the breaking of six ribs 6	of sword to Colonel	
" having served under	Wright . . . 25	
Colonel Cushing one	" one suit of gray clothes	
month . . . 44	(ingeniously unbecoming) . . . 15	
	" musical entertainments (drum and fife six months) . . . 5	
	" one dinner after return, 1	
	" chance of pension . 1	
	" privilege of drawing long bow during rest of natural life . . 23	
———	———	
100	100	

E. E.

It would appear that Mr. Sawin found the actual feast curiously the reverse of the bill of fare advertised in Faneuil Hall and other places. His primary object seems to have been the making of his fortune. *Quærenda pecunia primum, virtus post nummos.* He hoisted sail for Eldorado, and shipwrecked on Point Tribulation. *Quid non mortalia pectora cogis, auri sacra fames?* The speculation has sometimes crossed my mind, in that dreary interval of drought which intervenes between quarterly stipendiary showers, that Providence, by the creation of a money-tree, might have simplified wonderfully the sometimes perplexing problem of human life. We read of bread-trees, the butter for which lies ready-churned in Irish bogs. Milk-trees we are assured of in South

America, and stout Sir John Hawkins testifies to water-trees in the Canaries. Boot-trees bear abundantly in Lynn and elsewhere ; and I have seen, in the entries of the wealthy, hat-trees with a fair show of fruit. A family-tree I once cultivated myself, and found therefrom but a scanty yield, and that quite tasteless and innutritious. Of trees bearing men we are not without example ; as those in the park of Louis the Eleventh of France. Who has forgotten, moreover, that olive-tree, growing in the Athenian's back-garden, with its strange uxorious crop, for the general propagation of which, as of a new and precious variety, the philosopher Diogenes, hitherto uninterested in arboriculture, was so zealous ? In the *sylva* of our own Southern States, the females of my family have called my attention to the china-tree. Not to multiply examples, I will barely add to my list the birch-tree, in the smaller branches of which has been implanted so miraculous a virtue for communicating the Latin and Greek languages, and which may well, therefore, be classed among the trees producing necessaries of life, — *venerabile donum fatalis virgæ.* That money-trees existed in the golden age there want not prevalent reasons for our believing. For does not the old proverb, when it asserts that money does not grow on *every* bush, imply *a fortiori* that there were certain bushes which did produce it ? Again, there is another ancient saw to the effect that money is the *root* of all evil. From which two adages it may be safe to infer that the aforesaid species of tree first degenerated into a shrub, then absconded underground, and finally, in our iron age, vanished altogether. In favorable exposures it may be con-

jectured that a specimen or two survived to a great
age, as in the garden of the Hesperides ; and, indeed,
what else could that tree in the Sixth Æneid have
been, with a branch whereof the Trojan hero pro-
cured admission to a territory, for the entering of
which money is a surer passport than to a cer-
tain other more profitable (too) foreign kingdom ?
Whether these speculations of mine have any force
in them, or whether they will not rather, by most
readers, be deemed impertinent to the matter in hand,
is a question which I leave to the determination of
an indulgent posterity. That there were, in more
primitive and happier times, shops where money was
sold, — and that, too, on credit and at a bargain, — I
take to be matter of demonstration. For what but a
dealer in this article was that Æolus who supplied
Ulysses with motive power for his fleet in bags ?
What that Ericus, king of Sweden, who is said to
have kept the winds in his cap ? What, in more
recent times, those Lapland Nornas who traded in
favorable breezes ? All which will appear the more
clearly when we consider, that, even to this day, *rais-
ing the wind* is proverbial for raising money, and that
brokers and banks were invented by the Venetians at
a later period.

And now for the improvement of this digression.
I find a parallel to Mr. Sawin's fortune in an ad-
venture of my own. For, shortly after I had first
broached to myself the before-stated natural-histori-
cal and archæological theories, as I was passing, *hæc
negotia penitus mecum revolvens*, through one of the
obscure suburbs of our New England metropolis, my
eye was attracted by these words upon a sign-board,

— CHEAP CASH-STORE. Here was at once the confirmation of my speculations, and the substance of my hopes. Here lingered the fragment of a happier past, or stretched out the first tremulous organic filament of a more fortunate future. Thus glowed the distant Mexico to the eyes of Sawin, as he looked through the dirty pane of the recruiting-office window, or speculated from the summit of that mirage Pisgah which the imps of the bottle are so cunning in raising up. Already had my Alnaschar-fancy (even during that first half believing glance) expended in various useful directions the funds to be obtained by pledging the manuscript of a proposed volume of discourses. Already did a clock ornament the tower of the Jaalam meeting-house, a gift appropriately, but modestly, commemorated in the parish and town records, both, for now many years, kept by myself. Already had my son Seneca completed his course at the University. Whether, for the moment, we may not be considered as actually lording it over those Baratarias with the viceroyalty of which Hope invests us, and whether we are ever so warmly housed as in our Spanish castles, would afford matter of argument. Enough that I found that sign-board to be no other than a bait to the trap of a decayed grocer. Nevertheless, I bought a pound of dates (getting short weight by reason of immense flights of harpy flies who pursued and lighted upon their prey even in the very scales), which purchase I made, not only with an eye to the little ones at home, but also as a figurative reproof of that too frequent habit of my mind, which, forgetting the due order of chronology, will often persuade me that the happy sceptre of

Saturn is stretched over this Astræa-forsaken nineteenth century.

Having glanced at the ledger of Glory under the title *Sawin, B.*, let us extend our investigations, and discover if that instructive volume does not contain some charges more personally interesting to ourselves. I think we should be more economical of our resources, did we thoroughly appreciate the fact, that, whenever Brother Jonathan seems to be thrusting his hand into his own pocket, he is, in fact, picking ours. I confess that the late *muck* which the country has been running has materially changed my views as to the best method of raising revenue. If, by means of direct taxation, the bills for every extraordinary outlay were brought under our immediate eye, so that, like thrifty housekeepers, we could see where and how fast the money was going, we should be less likely to commit extravagances. At present, these things are managed in such a hugger-mugger way, that we know not what we pay for ; the poor man is charged as much as the rich ; and, while we are saving and scrimping at the spigot, the government is drawing off at the bung. If we could know that a part of the money we expend for tea and coffee goes to buy powder and balls, and that it is Mexican blood which makes the clothes on our backs more costly, it would set some of us athinking. During the present fall, I have often pictured to myself a government official entering my study and handing me the following bill : —

WASHINGTON, Sept. 30, 1848.

REV. HOMER WILBUR to 𝔘𝔫𝔠𝔩𝔢 𝔖𝔞𝔪𝔲𝔢𝔩,   Dr.

To his share of work done in Mexico on partnership account, sundry jobs, as below.

" killing, maiming, and wounding about 5,000 Mexicans	$2.00
" slaughtering one woman carrying water to wounded	.10
" extra work on two different Sabbaths (one bombardment and one assault) whereby the Mexicans were prevented from defiling themselves with the idolatries of high mass . . .	3.50
" throwing an especially fortunate and Protestant bombshell into the Cathedral at Vera Cruz, whereby several female Papists were slain at the altar	.50
" his proportion of cash paid for conquered territory	1.75
" do. do. for conquering do. .	1.50
" manuring do. with new superior compost called "American Citizen"	.50
" extending the area of freedom and Protestantism .	.01
" glory	.01
	———
	$9.87

Immediate payment is requested.

N. B. Thankful for former favors, U. S. requests a continuance of patronage. Orders executed with neatness and despatch. Terms as low as those of any other contractor for the same kind and style of work.

I can fancy the official answering my look of horror with "Yes, Sir, it looks like a high charge, Sir; but in these days slaughtering is slaughtering." Verily, I would that every one understood that it was; for it goes about obtaining money under the false pretence of being glory. For me, I have an imagination which plays me uncomfortable tricks. It happens to me sometimes to see a slaughterer on his way home from his day's work, and forthwith my imagination puts a cocked-hat upon his head and epaulettes upon his shoulders, and sets him up as a candidate for the Presidency. So, also, on a recent public occasion, as the place assigned to the "Reverend Clergy" is just behind that of "Officers of the Army and Navy" in processions, it was my fortune to be seated at the dinner-table over against one of these respectable persons. He was arrayed as (out of his own profession) only kings, court-officers, and footmen are in Europe, and Indians in America. Now what does my over-officious imagination but set to work upon him, strip him of his gay livery, and present him to me coatless, his trowsers thrust into the tops of a pair of boots thick with clotted blood, and a basket on his arm out of which lolled a gore-smeared axe, thereby destroying my relish for the temporal mercies upon the board before me ? — H. W.]

No. IX.

A THIRD LETTER FROM B. SAWIN, Esq.

[Upon the following letter slender comment will
be needful. In what river Selemnus has Mr. Sawin
bathed, that he has become so swiftly oblivious of
his former loves ? From an ardent and (as befits a
soldier) confident wooer of that coy bride, the popu-
lar favor, we see him subside of a sudden into the
(I trust not jilted) Cincinnatus, returning to his
plough with a goodly-sized branch of willow in his
hand ; figuratively returning, however, to a figura-
tive plough, and from no profound affection for that
honored implement of husbandry (for which, indeed,
Mr. Sawin never displayed any decided predilection),
but in order to be gracefully summoned therefrom
to more congenial labors. It would seem that the
character of the ancient Dictator had become part of
the recognized stock of our modern political comedy,
though, as our term of office extends to a quadrennial
length, the parallel is not so minutely exact as could
be desired. It is sufficiently so, however, for pur-
poses of scenic representation. An humble cottage
(if built of logs, the better) forms the Arcadian back-
ground of the stage. This rustic paradise is labelled
Ashland, Jaalam, North Bend, Marshfield, Kinder-
hook, or Baton Rouge, as occasion demands. Before
the door stands a something with one handle (the

other painted in proper perspective), which repre-
sents, in happy ideal vagueness, the plough.   To this
the defeated candidate rushes with delirious joy, wel-
comed as a father by appropriate groups of happy
laborers, or from it the successful one is torn with
difficulty, sustained alone by a noble sense of public
duty.   Only I have observed, that, if the scene be
laid at Baton Rouge or Ashland, the laborers are kept
carefully in the background, and are heard to shout
from behind the scenes in a singular tone resembling
ululation, and accompanied by a sound not unlike
vigorous clapping.   This, however, may be artisti-
cally in keeping with the habits of the rustic popula-
tion of those localities.   The precise connection be-
tween agricultural pursuits and statesmanship I have
not been able, after diligent inquiry, to discover.   But,
that my investigations may not be barren of all fruit,
I will mention one curious statistical fact, which I
consider thoroughly established, namely, that no real
farmer ever attains practically beyond a seat in Gen-
eral Court, however theoretically qualified for more
exalted station.

It is probable that some other prospect has been
opened to Mr. Sawin, and that he has not made this
great sacrifice without some definite understanding in
regard to a seat in the cabinet or a foreign mission.
It may be supposed that we of Jalaam were not un-
touched by a feeling of villatic pride in beholding our
townsman occupying so large a space in the public
eye.   And to me, deeply revolving the qualifications
necessary to a candidate in these frugal times, those
of Mr. S. seemed peculiarly adapted to a successful
campaign.   The loss of a leg, an arm, an eye, and

four fingers reduced him so nearly to the condition of a *vox et præterea nihil*, that I could think of nothing but the loss of his head by which his chance could have been bettered.   But since he has chosen to balk our suffrages, we must content ourselves with what we can get, remembering *lactucas non esse dandas, dum cardui sufficiant.* — H. W.]

I SPOSE you recollect that I explained my gennle
        views
In the last billet thet I writ, 'way down frum
        Veery Cruze,
Jest arter I 'd a kind o' ben spontanously sot up
To run unanimously fer the Presidential cup ;
O' course it wor n't no wish o' mine, 't wuz ferfle-
        ly distressin',
But poppiler enthusiasm gut so almighty pressin'
Thet, though like sixty all along I fumed an'
        fussed an' sorrered,
There did n't seem no ways to stop their bringin'
        on me forrerd :
Fact is, they udged the matter so, I could n't help
        admittin'
The Father o' his Country's shoes no feet but
        mine 'ould fit in,
Besides the savin' o' the soles fer ages to succeed,
Seein' thet with one wannut foot, a pair 'd be
        more 'n I need ;
An', tell ye wut, them shoes 'll want a thund'rin'
        sight o' patchin',
Ef this ere fashion is to last we 've gut into o'
        hatchin'

A pair o' second Washintons fer every new elec-
    tion, —
Though, fur ez number one's consarned, I don't
    make no objection.

I wuz agoin' on to say thet wen at fust I saw
The masses would stick to 't I wuz the Country's
    father-'n-law,
(They would ha' hed it *Father*, but I told 'em
    't would n't du,
Coz thet wuz sutthin' of a sort they could n't split
    in tu,
An' Washinton hed hed the thing laid fairly to
    his door,
Nor dars n't say 't worn't his'n, much ez sixty
    year afore,)
But 't aint no matter ez to thet; wen I wuz nom-
    ernated,
'T worn't natur but wut I should feel consid'able
    elated.
An' wile the hooraw o' the thing wuz kind o' noo
    an' fresh,
I thought our ticket would ha' caird the country
    with a resh.

Sence I 've come hum, though, an' looked round,
    I think I seem to find
Strong argiments ez thick ez fleas to make me
    change my mind;
It 's clear to any one whose brain ain't fur gone
    in a phthisis,

Thet hail Columby's happy land is goin' thru a
 crisis,

An' 't would n't noways du to hev the people's
 mind distracted

By bein' all to once by sev'ral pop'lar names
 attackted;

'T would save holl haycartloads o' fuss an' three
 four months o' jaw,

Ef some illustrous paytriot should back out an'
 withdraw;

So, ez I aint a crooked stick, jest like — like ole
 (I swow,

I dunno ez I know his name) — I 'll go back to
 my plough.

Now, 't aint no more 'n is proper 'n' right in sech
 a sitooation

To hint the course you think 'll be the savin' o'
 the nation;

To funk right out o' p'lit'cal strife ain't thought
 to be the thing,

Without you deacon off the toon you want your
 folks should sing;

So I edvise the noomrous friends thet 's in one
 boat with me

To jest up killock, jam right down their hellum
 hard a lee,

Haul the sheets taut, an', laying out upon the
 Suthun tack,

Make fer the safest port they can, wich, *I* think,
 is Ole Zack.

Next thing you 'll want to know, I spose, wut
    argimunts I seem
To see thet makes me think this ere 'll be the
    strongest team ;
Fust place, I 've ben consid'ble round in bar-
    rooms an' saloons
Agethrin' public sentiment, 'mongst Demmercrats
    and Coons,
An' 't aint ve'y offen thet I meet a chap but wut
    goes in
Fer Rough an' Ready, fair an' square, hufs, tal-
    ler, horns, an' skin ;
I don't deny but wut, fer one, ez fur ez I could
    see,
I did n't like at fust the Pheladelphy nomer-
    nee ;
I could ha pinted to a man thet wuz, I guess, a
    peg
Higher than him,— a soger, tu, an' with a wood-
    en leg ;
But every day with more an' more o' Taylor
    zeal I 'm burnin',
Seein' wich way the tide thet sets to office is
    aturnin',
Wy, into Bellers's we notched the votes down on
    three sticks, —
'T wuz Birdofredum *one*, Cass *aught*, an' Taylor
    twenty-six,
An', bein' the on'y canderdate thet wuz upon the
    ground,

They said 't wuz no more 'n right thet I should
    pay the drinks all round ;
Ef I 'd expected sech a trick, I would n't ha' cut
    my foot
By goin' an' votin' fer myself like a consumed
    coot.
It did n't make no diff'rence, though ; I wish I
    may be cust,
Ef Bellers wuz n't slim enough to say he would
    n't trust !

Another pint thet influences the minds o' sober
    jedges
Is thet the Gin'ral hez n't gut tied hand an' foot
    with pledges ;
He hez n't told ye wut he is, an' so there aint no
    knowin'
But wut he may turn out to be the best there is
    agoin' ;
This, at the o'ny spot thet pinched, the shoe di-
    rectly eases,
Coz every one is free to 'xpect percisely wut he
    pleases :
I want free-trade ; you don't ; the Gin'ral is n't
    bound to neither ; —
I vote my way ; you, yourn ; an' both air sooted
    to a T there.
Ole Rough an' Ready, tu, 's a Wig, but without
    bein' ultry
(He 's like a holsome hayinday, thet 's warm,
    but is n't sultry) ;

He 's jest wut I should call myself, a kin o'
    scratch, ez 't ware,
Thet aint exacly all a wig nor wholly your own
    hair ;
I 've ben a Wig three weeks myself, jest o' this
    mod'rate sort,
An' don't find them an' Demmercrats so differ-
    ent ez I thought ;
They both act pooty much alike, an' push an'
    scrouge an' cus ;
They 're like two pickpockets in league fer Un-
    cle Samwell's pus ;
Each takes a side, an' then they squeeze the old
    man in between 'em,
Turn all his pockets wrong side out an' quick ez
    lightnin' clean 'em ;
To nary one on 'em I 'd trust a secon'-handed
    rail
No furder off 'an I could sling a bullock by the
    tail.
Webster sot matters right in thet air Mashfiel'
    speech o' his'n ; —
" Taylor," sez he, "aint nary ways the one thet
    I 'd a chizzen,
Nor he aint fittin' fer the place, an' like ez not
    he aint
No more 'n a tough ole bullethead, an' no gret of
    a saint ;
But then," sez he, " obsarve my pint, he 's jest ez
    good to vote fer

Ez though the greasin' on him worn't a thing to
     hire Choate fer ;
Aint it ez easy done to drop a ballot in a
     box
Fer one ez 't is fer t' other, fer the bulldog ez the
     fox ? "
It takes a mind like Dannel's, fact, ez big ez all
     ou' doors
To find out thet it looks like rain arter it fairly
     pours ;
I 'gree with him, it aint so dreffle troublesome to
     vote
Fer Taylor arter all, — it 's jest to go an' change
     your coat ;
Wen he 's once greased, you 'll swaller him an'
     never know on 't, scurce,
Unless he scratches, goin' down, with them air
     Gin'ral's spurs.

I 've ben a votin' Demmercrat, ez reg'lar ez a
     clock,
But don't find goin' Taylor gives my narves no
     gret 'f a shock ;
Truth is, the cutest leadin' Wigs, ever sence fust
     they found
Wich side the bread gut buttered on, hev kep'
     a edgin' round ;
They kin' o' slipt the planks frum out th' ole
     platform one by one,
An' made it gradooally noo, 'fore folks know'd
     wut wuz done,

Till, fur 'z I know, there aint an inch thet I could
    lay my han' on,
But I, or any Demmercrat, feels comf'table to
    stan' on,
An' ole Wig doctrines act'lly look, their occ'pants
    bein gone,
Lonesome ez staddles on a mash without no hay-
    ricks on.

I spose it 's time now I should give my thoughts
    upon the plan,
Thet chipped the shell at Buffalo, o' settin' up
    ole Van.
I used to vote fer Martin, but, I swan, I 'm clean
    disgusted, —
He aint the man thet I can say is fittin' to be
    trusted ;
He aint half antislav'ry 'nough, nor I aint sure,
    ez some be,
He 'd go in fer abolishin' the Deestrick o' Co-
    lumby ;
An', now I come to recollect, it kin' o' makes me
    sick 'z
A horse, to think o' wut he wuz in eighteen
    thirty-six.
An' then, another thing ; — I guess, though
    mebby I am wrong,
This Buff'lo plaster aint agoin' to dror almighty
    strong ;
Some folks, I know, hev gut th' idee thet No-
    'thun dough 'll rise,

Though, 'fore I see it riz an' baked, I would n't
    trust my eyes ;
'T will take more emptins, a long chalk, than
    this noo party 's gut,
To give sech heavy cakes ez them a start, I tell
    ye wut.
But even ef they caird the day, there would n't
    be no endurin'
To stand upon a platform with sech critters ez
    Van Buren ; —
An' his son John, tu, I can't think how thet air
    chap should dare
To speak ez he doos; wy, they say he used to
    cuss an' swear !
I spose he never read the hymn thet tells how
    down the stairs
A feller with long legs wuz throwed thet would
    n't say his prayers.

This brings me to another pint: the leaders o'
    the party
Aint jest sech men ez I can act along with free
    an' hearty ;
They aint not quite respectable, an' wen a fel-
    ler's morrils
Don't toe the straightest kin' o' mark, wy, him
    an' me jest quarrils.
I went to a free soil meetin' once, an' wut d' ye
    think I see ?
A feller wuz aspoutin' there thet act'lly come to
    me,

About two year ago last spring, ez nigh ez I can
jedge
An' axed me ef I did n't want to sign the Tem-
prunce pledge!
He's one o' them thet goes about an' sez you
hed n't ough' to
Drink nothin', mornin', noon, or night, stronger
'an Taunton water.
There's one rule I 've ben guided by, in settlin'
how to vote, ollers, —
I take the side thet *is n't* took by them consarned
teetotallers.

Ez fer the niggers, I 've ben South, an' thet hez
changed my mind ;
A lazier, more ungrateful set you could n't no-
wers find.
You know I mentioned in my last thet I should
buy a nigger,
Ef I could make a purchase at a pooty mod'rate
figger ;
So, ez there's nothin' in the world I 'm fonder
of 'an gunnin',
I closed a bargin finally to take a feller runnin'.
I shou'dered queen's-arm an' stumped out, an'
wen I come t' th' swamp,
'T worn't very long afore I gut upon the nest o'
Pomp ;
I come acrost a kin' o' hut, an', playin' round
the door,

Some little woolly-headed cubs, ez many 'z six or
　　more
At fust I thought o' firin', but *think twice* is saf-
　　est ollers :
There aint, thinks I, not one on em' but 's wuth
　　his twenty dollars,
Or would be, ef I hed 'em back into a Christian
　　land, —
How temptin' all on 'em would look upon an
　　auction-stand !
(Not but wut *I* hate Slavery in th' abstract, stem
　　to starn, —
I leave it ware our fathers did, a privit State
　　consarn.)
Soon 'z they see me, they yelled an' run, but
　　Pomp wuz out ahoein'
A leetle patch o' corn he hed, or else there aint
　　no knowin'
He would n't ha' took a pop at me ; but I hed
　　gut the start,
An' wen he looked, I vow he groaned ez though
　　he 'd broke his heart ;
He done it like a wite man, tu, ez nat'ral ez a
　　pictur,
The imp'dunt, pis'nous hypocrite ! wus 'an a boy
　　constrictur.
" You can't gum *me*, I tell ye now, an' so you
　　need n't try,
I 'xpect my eye-teeth every mail, so jest shet
　　up," sez I.

" Don't go to actin' ugly now, or else I 'll jest let
    strip,
You 'd best draw kindly, seein' 'z how I 've gut
    ye on the hip ;
Besides, you darned ole fool, it aint no gret of a
    disaster
To be benev'lently druv back to a contented mas-
    ter,
Ware you hed Christian priv'ledges you don't
    seem quite aware of,
Or you 'd ha' never run away from bein' well
    took care of ;
Ez fer kin' treatment, wy, he wuz so fond on ye,
    he said
He 'd give a fifty spot right out, to git ye, 'live
    or dead ;
Wite folks aint sot by half ez much ; 'member I
    run away,
Wen I wuz bound to Cap'n Jakes, to Matty-
    squmscot bay ;
Don' know him, likely ? Spose not : wal, the
    mean ole codger went
An' offered — wut reward, think ? Wal, it
    worn't no *less* 'n a cent."

Wal, I jest gut 'em into line, an druv 'em on
    afore me,
The pis'nous brutes, I 'd no idee o' the ill-will
    they bore me ;
We walked till som'ers about noon, an' then it
    grew so hot

I thought it best to camp awile, so I chose out a
    spot

Jest under a magnoly tree, an' there right down
    I sot ;

Then I unstrapped my wooden leg, coz it begun
    to chafe,

An' laid it down jest by my side, supposin' all
    wuz safe ;

I made my darkies all set down around me in a
    ring,

An' sot an' kin' o' ciphered up how much the lot
    would bring ;

But, wile I drinked the peaceful cup of a pure
    heart an' mind,

(Mixed with some wiskey, now an' then,) Pomp
    he snaked up behind,

An', creepin grad'lly close tu, ez quiet ez a
    mink,

Jest grabbed my leg, and then pulled foot,
    quicker 'an you could wink,

An', come to look, they each on 'em hed gut
    behin' a tree,

An' Pomp poked out the leg a piece, jest so ez I
    could see,

An' yelled to me to throw away my pistils an'
    my gun,

Or else thet they 'd cair off the leg an' fairly cut
    the run.

I vow I did n't b'lieve there wuz a decent alli-
    gatur

Thet hed a heart so destitoot o' common human
  natur ;

However, ez there wor n't no help, I finally give
  in

An' heft my arms away to git my leg safe back
  agin.

Pomp gethered all the weapins up, an' then he
  come an' grinned,

He showed his ivory some, I guess, an' sez, "You
  're fairly pinned ;

Jest buckle on your leg agin, an' git right up an'
  come,

'T wun't du fer fammerly men like me to be so
  long from hum."

At fust I put my foot right down an' swore I
  would n't budge.

" Jest ez you choose," sez he, quite cool, " either
  be shot or trudge."

So this black-hearted monster took an' act'lly
  druv me back

Along the very feetmarks o' my happy mornin'
  track,

An' kep' me pris'ner 'bout six months, an' worked
  me, tu, like sin,

Till I hed gut his corn an' his Carliny taters
  in ;

He made me larn him readin', tu, (although the
  crittur saw

How much it hut my morril sense to act agin the
  law,)

So 'st he could read a Bible he 'd gut ; an' axed
    ef I could pint
The North Star out; but there I put his nose
    some out o' jint,
Fer I weeled roun' about sou'west, an', lookin' up
    a bit,
Picked out a middlin' shiny one an' tole him thet
    wuz it.
Fin'lly, he took me to the door, an', givin' me a
    kick,
Sez, " Ef you know wut 's best fer ye, be off,
    now, double-quick ;
The winter-time 's a comin' on, an', though I gut
-    ye cheap,
You 're so darned lazy, I don't think you 're
    hardly wuth your keep ;
Besides, the childrin 's growin' up, an' you aint
    jest the model
I 'd like to hev 'em immertate, an' so you 'd bet-
    ter toddle ! "

Now is there any thin' on airth 'll ever prove to
    me
Thet renegader slaves like him air fit fer bein'
    free ?
D' you think they 'll suck me in to jine the
    Buff'lo chaps, an' them
Rank infidels thet go agin the Scriptur'l cus o'
    Shem ?
Not by a jugfull ! sooner 'n thet, I 'd go thru
    fire an' water :

Wen I hev once made up my mind, a meet'nhus
    aint sotter;
No, not though all the crows thet flies to pick my
    bones wuz cawin', —
I guess we 're in a Christian land, —
       Yourn,
          BIRDOFREDUM SAWIN.

[Here, patient reader, we take leave of each other,
I trust with some mutual satisfaction. I say *patient*,
for I love not that kind which skims dippingly over
the surface of the page, as swallows over a pool
before rain. By such no pearls shall be gathered.
But if no pearls there be (as, indeed, the world is not
without example of books wherefrom the longest-
winded diver shall bring up no more than his proper
handful of mud), yet let us hope that an oyster or
two may reward adequate perseverance. If neither
pearls nor oysters, yet is patience itself a gem worth
diving deeply for.

It may seem to some that too much space has been
usurped by my own private lucubrations, and some
may be fain to bring against me that old jest of him
who preached all his hearers out of the meeting-
house save only the sexton, who, remaining for yet a
little space, from a sense of official duty, at last gave
out also, and, presenting the keys, humbly requested
our preacher to lock the doors, when he should have
wholly relieved himself of his testimony. I confess
to a satisfaction in the self act of preaching, nor do I
esteem a discourse to be wholly thrown away even
upon a sleeping or unintelligent auditory. I cannot
easily believe that the Gospel of Saint John, which

Jacques Cartier ordered to be read in the Latin
tongue to the Canadian savages, upon his first meet-
ing with them, fell altogether upon stony ground.
For the earnestness of the preacher is a sermon ap-
preciable by dullest intellects and most alien ears.
In this wise did Episcopius convert many to his opin-
ions, who yet understood not the language in which
he discoursed.   The chief thing is, that the mes-
senger believe that he has an authentic message to
deliver.   For counterfeit messengers that mode of
treatment which Father John de Plano Carpini re-
lates to have prevailed among the Tartars would
seems effectual, and, perhaps, deserved enough.   For
my own part, I may lay claim to so much of the
spirit of martyrdom as would have led me to go into
banishment with those clergymen whom Alphonso
the Sixth of Portugal drave out of his kingdom for
refusing to shorten their pulpit eloquence.   It is pos-
sible, that, having been invited into my brother Big-
low's desk, I may have been too little scrupulous in
using it for the venting of my own peculiar doctrines
to a congregation drawn together in the expectation
and with the desire of hearing him.

  I am not wholly unconscious of a peculiarity of men-
tal organization which impels me, like the railroad-
engine with its train of cars, to run backward for a
short distance in order to obtain a fairer start.   I may
compare myself to one fishing from the rocks when
the sea runs high, who, misinterpreting the suction of
the under-tow for the biting of some larger fish, jerks
suddenly, and finds that he has *caught bottom*, hauling
in upon the end of his line a trail of various *algœ*,
among which, nevertheless, the naturalist may haply
find somewhat to repay the disappointment of the

angler. Yet have I conscientiously endeavored to adapt myself to the impatient temper of the age, daily degenerating more and more from the high standard of our pristine New England. To the catalogue of lost arts I would mournfully add also that of listening to two-hour sermons. Surely we have been abridged into a race of pigmies. For, truly, in those of the old discourses yet subsisting to us in print, the endless spinal column of divisions and subdivisions can be likened to nothing so exactly as to the vertebræ of the saurians, whence the theorist may conjecture a race of Anakim proportionate to the withstanding of these other monsters. I say Anakim rather than Nephelim, because there seem reasons for supposing that the race of those whose heads (though no giants) are constantly enveloped in clouds (which that name imports) will never become extinct. The attempt to vanquish the innumerable *heads* of one of those aforementioned discourses may supply us with a plausible interpretation of the second labor of Hercules, and his successful experiment with fire affords us a useful precedent.

But while I lament the degeneracy of the age in this regard, I cannot refuse to succumb to its influence. Looking out through my study-window, I see Mr. Biglow at a distance busy in gathering his Baldwins, of which, to judge by the number of barrels lying about under the trees, his crop is more abundant than my own, — by which sight I am admonished to turn to those orchards of the mind wherein my labors may be more prospered, and apply myself diligently to the preparation of my next Sabbath's discourse. — H. W.]

GLOSSARY.

A.

Act'lly, *actually.*
Air, *are.*
Airth, *earth.*
Airy, *area.*
Aree, *area.*
Arter, *after.*
Ax, *ask.*

B.

Beller, *bellow.*
Bellowses, *lungs.*
Ben, *been.*
Bile, *boil.*
Bimeby, *by and by.*
Blurt out, *to speak bluntly.*
Bust, *burst.*
Buster, *a roistering blade;* used also as a general superlative.

C.

Caird, *carried.*
Cairn, *carrying.*
Caleb, *a turncoat.*
Cal'late, *calculate.*
Cass, *a person with two lives.*
Close, *clothes.*
Cockerel, *a young cock.*
Cocktail, *a kind of drink;* also, *an ornament peculiar to soldiers.*
Convention, *a place where people are imposed on; a juggler's show.*
Coons, *a cant term for a now defunct party;* derived, perhaps, from the fact of their being commonly *up a tree.*
Cornwallis, *a sort of muster in* masquerade; supposed to have had its origin soon after the Revolution, and to commemorate the surrender of Lord Cornwallis. It took the place of the old Guy Fawkes procession.
Crooked stick, *a perverse, froward person.*
Cunnle, *a colonel.*
Cus, *a curse;* also, *a pitiful fellow.*

D.

Darsn't, used indiscriminately, either in singular or plural number, for *dare not, dares not,* and *dared not.*
Deacon off, *to give the cue to;* derived from a custom, once universal, now extinct, in our New England Congregational churches. An important part of the office of deacon was to read aloud the hymns *given out* by the minister, one line at a time, the congregation singing each line as soon as read.
Demmercrat, leadin', *one in favor of extending slavery; a free-trade lecturer maintained in the custom-house.*
Desput, *desperate.*
Doos, *does.*
Doughface, *a contented lick-spittle;* a common variety of Northern politician.
Dror, *draw.*
Du, *do.*
Dunno, dno, *do not* or *does not know.*
Dut, *Dirt.*

E.

Eend, *end.*
Ef, *if.*
Emptins, *yeast.*
Env'y, *envoy.*
Everlasting, an intensive, without reference to duration.
Ev'y, *every.*
Ez, *as.*

F.

Fer, *for.*
Ferfle, ferful, *fearful;* also an intensive.
Fin', *find.*
Fish-skin, used in New England to clarify coffee.
Fix, *a difficulty, a nonplus.*
Foller, folly, *to follow.*
Forrerd, *forward.*
Frum, *from.*
Fur, *far.*
Furder, *farther.*
Furrer, *furrow.* Metaphorically, *to draw a straight furrow* is to live uprightly or decorously.
Fust, *first.*

G.

Gin, *gave.*
Git, *get.*
Gret, *great.*
Grit, *spirit, energy, pluck.*
Grout, *to sulk.*
Grouty, *crabbed, surly.*
Gum, *to impose on.*
Gump, *a foolish fellow, a dullard.*
Gut, *got.*

H.

Hed, *had.*
Heern, *heard.*
Hellum, *helm.*
Hendy, *handy.*
Het, *heated.*
Hev, *have.*
Hez, *has.*
Holl, *whole.*
Holt, *hold.*
Huf, *hoof.*

Hull, *whole.*
Hum, *home.*
Humbug, *General Taylor's anti-slavery.*
Hut, *hurt.*

I.

Idno, *I do not know.*
In'my, *enemy.*
Insines, *ensigns;* used to designate both the officer who carries the standard, and the standard itself.
Inter, intu, *into.*

J.

Jedge, *judge.*
Jest, *just.*
Jine, *join.*
Jint, *joint.*
Junk, *a fragment of any solid substance.*

K.

Keer, *care.*
Kep, *kept.*
Killock, *a small anchor.*
Kin', kin' o', kinder, *kind, kind of.*

L.

Lawth, *loath.*
Let day-light into, *to shoot.*
Let on, *to hint, to confess, to own.*
Lick, *to beat, to overcome.*
Lights, *the bowels.*
Lily-pads, *leaves of the water-lily.*
Long-sweetening, *molasses.*

M.

Mash, *marsh.*
Mean, *stingy, ill-natured.*
Min', *mind.*

N.

Ninepunce, *ninepence, twelve and a half cents.*
Nowers, *nowhere.*

O.

Offen, *often.*
Ole, *old.*
Ollers, olluz, *always.*
On, *of;* used before *it* or *them,* or at the end of a sentence, as, *on't, on 'em, nut ez ever I heerd on.*
On'y, *only.*
Ossifer, *officer* (seldom heard).

P.

Peaked, *pointed.*
Peek, *to peep.*
Pickerel, *the pike, a fish.*
Pint, *point.*
Pocket full of rocks, *plenty of money.*
Pooty, *pretty.*
Pop'ler, *conceited, popular.*
Pus, *purse.*
Put out, *troubled, vexed.*

Q.

Quarter, *a quarter-dollar.*
Queen's arm, *a musket.*

R.

Resh, *rush.*
Revelee, *the réveille.*
Rile, *to trouble.*
Riled, *angry; disturbed,* as the sediment in any liquid.
Riz, *risen.*
Row, a long row to hoe, *a difficult task.*
Rugged, *robust.*

S.

Sarse, *abuse, impertinence.*
Sartin, *certain.*
Saxon, *sacristan, sexton.*
Scaliest, *worst.*
Scringe, *cringe.*
Scrouge, *to crowd.*
Sech, *such.*
Set by, *valued.*
Shakes, great, *of considerable consequence.*

Shappoes, *chapeaux, cocked-hats.*
Sheer, *share.*
Shet, *shut.*
Shut, *shirt.*
Skeered, *scared.*
Skeeter, *mosquito.*
Skooting, *running,* or *moving swiftly.*
Slarterin', *slaughtering.*
Slim, *contemptible.*
Snaked, *crawled like a snake;* but *to snake any one out* is to track him to his hiding-place; *to snake a thing out* is to snatch it out.
Soffies, *sofas.*
Sogerin', *soldiering;* a barbarous amusement common among men in the savage state.
Som'ers, *somewhere.*
So 'st, *so as that.*
Sot, *set, obstinate, resolute.*
Spiles, *spoils; objects of political ambition.*
Spry, *active.*
Staddles, *stout stakes driven into salt marshes,* on which the hayricks are set, and thus raised out of the reach of high tides.
Streaked, *uncomfortable, discomfited.*
Suckle, *circle.*
Sutthin', *something.*
Suttin, *certain.*

T.

Take on, *to sorrow.*
Talents, *talons.*
Taters, *potatoes.*
Tell, *till.*
Tetch, *touch.*
Tetch tu, *to be able;* used always after a negative in this sense.
Tollable, *tolerable.*
Toot, used derisively for *playing on any wind instrument.*
Thru, *through.*
Thundering, a euphemism common in New England, for the profane English expression *devilish.* Perhaps derived from the belief, common formerly, that thunder was caused by the Prince of the Air, for some of whose accomplishments consult Cotton Mather.

Tu, *to, too;* commonly has this sound when used emphatically, or at the end of a sentence. At other times it has a sound of *t* in *tough*, as, *Ware ye goin' tu? Goin' tu Boston.*

U.

Ugly, *ill-tempered, intractable.*

Uncle Sam, *United States;* the largest boaster of liberty and owner of slaves.

Unrizzest, applied to dough or bread; *heavy, most unrisen, or most incapable of rising.*

V.

V spot, *a five-dollar bill.*

Vally, *value.*

W.

Wake snakes, *to get into trouble.*

Wal, *well;* spoken with great deliberation, and sometimes with the *a* very much flattened, sometimes (but more seldom) very much broadened.

Wannut, *walnut (hickory).*

Ware, *where.*

Ware, *were.*

Whopper, *an uncommonly large lie;* as, that General Taylor is in favor of the Wilmot Proviso.

Wig, *Whig;* a party now dissolved.

Wunt, *will not.*

Wus, *worse.*

Wut, *what.*

Wuth, *worth;* as, *Antislavery perfessions 'fore 'lection aint wuth a Bungtown copper.*

Wuz, *was,* sometimes *were.*

Y.

Yaller, *yellow.*

Yeller, *yellow.*

Yellars, *a disease of peach-trees.*

Z.

Zach, Ole, *a second Washington, an antislavery slaveholder, a humane buyer and seller of men and women, a Christian hero generally.*

INDEX.

—◆—

A.

A. B., information wanted concerning, 130.

Adam, eldest son of, respected, 60.

Æneas goes to hell, 157.

Æolus, a seller of money, as is supposed by some, 157.

Æschylus, a saying of, 104, *note*.

Alligator, a decent one conjectured to be, in some sort, humane, 176.

Alphonso the Sixth of Portugal, tyrannical act of, 180.

Ambrose, Saint, excellent (but rationalistic) sentiment of, 86.

"American Citizen," new compost so called, 160.

American Eagle, a source of inspiration, 96 — hitherto wrongly classed, 104 — long bill of, *ib.*

Amos, cited, 85.

Anakim, that they formerly existed, shown, 181.

Angels, providentially speak French, 73 — conjectured to be skilled in all tongues, *ib.*

Anglo-Saxondom, its idea, what, 70.

Anglo-Saxon mask, 71.

Anglo-Saxon race, 66.

Anglo-Saxon verse, by whom carried to perfection, 61.

Antonius, a speech of, 91 — by whom best reported, *ib.*

Apocalypse, beast in, magnetic to theologians, 137.

Apollo, confessed mortal by his own oracle, 137.

Apollyon, his tragedies popular, 126.

Appian, an Alexandrian, not equal to Shakspeare as an orator, 91.

Ararat, ignorance of foreign tongues is an, 106.

Arcadian background, 162.

Aristophanes, 84.

Arms, profession of, once esteemed especially that of gentlemen, 60.

Arnold, 93.

Ashland, 162.

Astor, Jacob, a rich man, 146.

Astræa, nineteenth century forsaken by, 59.

Athenians, ancient, an institution of, 92.

Atherton, Senator, envies the loon, 114.

Austin, St., profane wish of, 94, *note*.

Aye-Aye, the, an African animal, America supposed to be settled by, 75.

B.

Babel, probably the first Congress, 105 — a gabble-mill, *ib.*

Baby, a low-priced one, 154.

Bagowind, Hon. Mr., whether to be damned, 117.

Baldwin apples, 181.

Baratarias, real or imaginary, which most pleasant, 158.

Barnum, a great natural curiosity recommended to, 101.

Barrels, an inference from seeing, 181.

Bâton Rouge, 162 — strange peculiarities of laborers at, 163.

Baxter, R., a saying of, 86.

Bay, Mattysqumscot, 175.

C.